Lessons
from the
Mahabharat
Greatest Spiritual Wisdom

PRANAY

BEL!EF

Published by

FiNGERPRINT! BEL!EF

An imprint of Prakash Books India Pvt. Ltd.

113/A, Darya Ganj, New Delhi-110 002,
Tel: (011) 2324 7062 – 65, Fax: (011) 2324 6975
Email: info@prakashbooks.com/sales@prakashbooks.com

facebook www.facebook.com/fingerprintpublishing
twitter www.twitter.com/FingerprintP
www.fingerprintpublishing.com

ISBN: 978 93 5440 078 0

Processed & printed in India

To a brilliant poet friend
Ipsita Ganguli

Preface

With the great Lord Ganesha as his scribe, the sage (*rishi*) Krishna Dwaipayan Vyasa composed the Mahabharat thousands of years ago. It is the longest epic poem in existence. Along with the Ramayan, the Mahabharat is the great *itihasa* (epic), teaching us the mystical *uttam rahasya* (greatest secrets) to fulfil our lives.

The stories and legends of the epic are weaved into the cultural fabric of the entire Indian subcontinent (called "Bharat" since ancient times) as well as in various other parts of Asia. Its enduring tales have been sung by bards and minstrels over millennia. Even the smallest sutra in the Mahabharat has immense lessons to teach!

Capturing the very essence of human existence, the Mahabharat is all-encompassing. It tells us how we are to play our own roles or parts on this earth, and within our universe of such great beauty, such tremendous energies. All the dimensions of life are brought together in the Mahabharat. It offers a priceless treasure of spiritual keys, teaching us how we can function with the totality of our energy and wisdom, especially during difficult situations and moments of crisis.

The aim of my book is to offer the finest life lessons from the Mahabharat, that guide us towards finding the greatness within our own souls. To know oneself at the level of soul is the highest revelation, sparking the awareness of our reality as spiritual beings dealing with material circumstances! It is ultimately all about enriching ourselves inwardly, and thereby moving towards truly successful, fearless living.

The Mahabharat is a work of great insight. It talks about the dualities of life: happiness and sorrow, good times and bad times, war and peace, belief and disbelief, enmity and friendship, honour and dishonour, loyalty and treachery, betrayal and valour, life and death, man and God! In that way, it is the ultimate must-have guide for us to be able to traverse the journey of life in a state of wonder, happiness, delight, and most importantly, courage or strength, so that we can maximize our potential as human beings.

Hari Om Tat Sat

Pranay

Contents

CHAPTER - 1

Essential Spiritual Objectives and Concepts

The Mahabharat is a life-manual for yogic living. It teaches us how to live with *santosha* (contentment), *atma-bal* (soulful strength), *dhairya/virya* (the attitudes of courage, boldness, and fortitude), and *akhanda-ananda* (uninterrupted bliss). It guides us on our spiritual quest for enlightened living.

True fulfilment, well-being, inner power, and strength are difficult to achieve without making spiritual or mystic truth the centre of our very existence. The

Mahabharat takes us towards well-being on both spheres: the material and the mystical. Wellness in both worldly and inward levels of being is its key objective. It takes us from *bhraanti* (wrong notions) towards *shaanti* (inner peace). The eventual aim and objective of the Mahabharat is to take us towards the spiritually awakened (*jaagrat*) state, and help us achieve union with ultimate reality (Brahman) or *Ishvara* (the Divine).

The Mahabharat is ultimately a text on spiritual and mystic truth, yet it also talks about myriad aspects of man's existence. Its lessons are meant to enrich us from within, at the level of the soul. It is rich with sublime spiritual tenets that the great rishis (ancient sages) wanted us to imbibe, internalize, and implement in our lives. The rishis had clear objectives for us, and through understanding these objectives, we attain clarity about what the Mahabharat actually means. Through the following concepts, it becomes evident that this epic abounds with spiritual secrets, which function as master keys to dealing with and overcoming any challenge in life:

Dharma

The first stanza of the great scripture the Bhagvad Gita, within the Mahabharat, contains the words *Dharmakshetre Kurukshetre*: "On the field of dharma, at Kurukshetra . . ." The concept of dharma or spiritual duty pervades the very core of the Mahabharat! The epic's objective is to educate us about our spiritual duty, which is to first of all follow our innermost nature and highest spiritual energy, under all circumstances. If one follows one's spiritual self-nature and thereby abides by dharma, every problem can be overcome. It is dharma that is our real strength, it is dharma from which all virtues arise. Even at the risk of endangering yourself, it is better to do your dharma than to follow someone else's nature (which would be *adharma* or non-dharma).

The prime instruction on dharma in the Mahabharat is Lord Krishna's advice to Arjun to recognize his self-nature of being a warrior, and to expend his entire energy in utilizing that towards a just cause! That is the essence of the Bhagvad Gita. The very idea of the divine Krishna being Arjun's charioteer is significant: telling us that our guide or divine driver towards dharma is indeed the Lord who resides deep within our own hearts.

And through the many stories within the Mahabharat, we again keep seeing this emphasis on dharma: for example, in the incident of *Yaksha Prashna*, where Yudhishthir brings his brothers back to life by successfully answering questions on true dharma posed by a *yaksha* (who turns out to be Yama/Dharmaraja, the Lord of Death and Dharma, and is Yudhishthir's divine father). Another incident, that of the Pandavs rescuing their arch-enemy cousin Duryodhan from King Chitrasena and the Gandharvas, demonstrates the true spirit of dharma: selfless, non-egoistic, and unclouded by personal like or dislike.

To attain dharma and *dharmic* action, first the superficial ego has to be dropped: in the Mahabharat, we see how Lord Hanuman specifically teaches both Arjun and Bheem (on two separate occasions) lessons in humility, thereby taking them towards utilizing their strength/skill as warriors for a dharmic cause and not personal aggrandizement!

The Mahabharat enlightens us about dharma not just at a mystical level, but also at a practical level (dharmic action). For example, it says, "*Dharmādarthaśca kāmaśca sa kimartham na sēvyatē"* meaning that from Dharma and from true righteousness comes material wealth, comes pleasure, and so on. In other words, by investing in dharmic or righteous action, one brings about both material and spiritual well-being.

The Mahabharat is a collation of the greatest spiritual teachings to have ever existed. The central idea of dharma or dharmic action echoes throughout this text. In fact, this idea is also at the centre of the other great Indian epic, the Ramayan. Dharma—and the actions generated through following the path of dharma—is considered the most profound phenomenon, taking you towards self-realization. The prime objective of the Mahabharat is to kindle the light of dharma within you. Dharma leads to *dhairya* (courage and true boldness). This leads us towards enlightenment (achieving *bodhi-chitta*).

Vidya

The Mahabharat teaches the highest spiritual knowledge (*para-vidya*) as well as knowledge to function in practical life. It condenses the keys of *yoga-darshana* (yogic philosophy) and *yoga-abhyasa* (yogic practice), helping us understand and practise both, no matter what one's path or work in life!

A key objective of the Mahabharat is for us to become established in *vidya* or wisdom. It encompasses both the greatest spiritual wisdom as well as intellectual and practical knowledge for dealing with material life. Krishna in fact bridges both aspects of wisdom: how to be completely dynamic in practical action, yet completely detached in our inward spiritual demeanour and wisdom!

From the spiritual angle, true wisdom or knowledge involves seeing the temporary nature of all material circumstances, and therefore not letting the mind get carried away by the thoughts of those. We must understand that neither painful nor pleasurable circumstances are our ultimate reality. They are simply a reflection of the divine cosmic play (or *Leela*) of the Infinite.

We must become more established in the deeper truth of our spiritual existence. This is comprised of pure consciousness-truth-bliss or *Sat-Chit-Ananda,* with Ananda or spiritual bliss/joy being our ultimate reality. This is the highest wisdom: the Mahabharat aims at making us realize the value of life and becoming blissful through it.

Becoming conscious of our inherent spiritual wisdom, we become more capable of dealing with difficult situations in life.

Intuitive Wisdom

Your intuition is a shrine where the Divine always dwells. Rest within the boundless power of your intuition and draw on it even more when the going gets tough. That is when it is needed the most. Don't look at life through the prism of thoughts/ intellect and feelings alone.

Your true wisdom is in your infinite storehouse of intuition: tap into it more! The Mahabharat's life lessons imbue us with the understanding that the energy-field of our intuition carries the energy of the Divine itself, and is our true reality. Don't get lost in the mental constructs of your own making, nor in fluctuating moods, for those are often a reflection of *maya* or illusion.

Through the intuitive perspective, we can deal with problems with greater poise, confidence, and inner power. We must awaken our intuitive "eye of wisdom" (*gyaana-chakshu/ divya-drishti*) within: this is key to the Mahabharat's objectives for us on our own life journeys.

Non-Anger

Time and again, the Mahabharat reminds us that non-agitation and non-anger (*akrodha*) are key to dealing with all crises. The angry mind cannot be a dwelling place of the Divine. The overly aggressive mind falls into self-destruction. Be balanced, be steady. Have tolerance: don't get carried away by moods or whimsical feelings/thoughts. Through trust and faith in yourself, cultivate tolerance even in the face of insults. This allows you to move towards truly courageous and dynamic living, ultimately culminating in finding the *Satyam-Shivam-Sundaram* or truth-goodness-beauty within life.

Follow the Yogis

Ideate and emulate the example of great yogis, rishis, and mystics. They exemplify both the spiritual and material glory of true yoga. Great people—those we can emulate—are known as *adarsha purusha*, and we must strive to learn from numerous such yogis/ sages and heroes/warriors/personalities within the Mahabharat.

Always remember this: within yourself, you have the capacity to be a true yogi! It's simply a question of looking deeper into your being and tapping into your deepest layer—where resides your truly divine self-potential.

The Mahabharat is a great repository of legends, anecdotes, and wisdom stories about yogis/rishis/ sages of the ancient civilization. The very ideation of the lives of the great spiritual pathfinders— and of the problems they often had to face—will imbue you with massive power and courage from within. Their vibe is real and palpable. Tap into that through subtle ideation in the core of your mind (no particular *prayer* is needed as such).

Cultivate the yogic attitude in all things. The basis of yoga philosophy and mysticism is cultivation of the priceless things in life: love towards work and towards all beings, and valuing the spiritual dimensions of yourself. These attributes fill us with tremendous self-power, integrity, and the ability to realize our highest potential. All this helps us awaken and unleash the greatest power of our consciousness in all that we do.

Tranquillity and Calmness

Establish your inner self in tranquil calmness (the state of *sama*). To be in a state of inner peace (*shaanti*) amidst all situations, is the most important spiritual secret for truly successful living.

Cultivating tranquillity and calmness of mind is real spiritual practice. It is the basis of all spiritual endeavour (*sadhana*) and imbues us with the strength needed to face various circumstances and situations, while being detached and blissfully happy within! It is the simple mystic principle of all the ages, most eloquently expressed through the various aspects of the Mahabharat.

True and great warriors always exhibit such tranquillity. If we look at the greatest warriors within the Mahabharat, we can observe that they are calm and non-possessive, and hence are ready to give their best energy to the battle at hand!

Eventually, the epic takes us back to the centre of our own spiritual being: from where arise the virtues of stillness, steadfastness, mental quietness, and ultimate dynamism. It is about mental equilibrium, which makes us truly joyful, creative, appreciative, and capable of understanding as well as dealing with all the varying circumstances of life.

The Infinite

The idea of infinity is firmly conveyed in the Mahabharat. Existence is *anaadi-ananta* (without beginning or end), and there resides an *ananta jyotih* (infinite divine light) within our own souls. Pay attention to this light within yourself.

No matter where you are stuck, if you contemplate the Infinite, you begin enjoying the fullest extent of human life. This contemplation generates power (*bala*) and love (*prema*), connecting you more deeply to the cosmos.

From the Mahabharat's point of view, each of us can be a seer of infinite truth: we have within us the greatest potential in seed form. All we need to essentially do is remove the lens of conditioned thoughts and prejudices about ourselves and the world, and thereby walk and act with bold faith, sureness, and decisiveness. We are children of the Divine Infinite. Remember this whenever you feel hopeless or low. This was the great Krishna's counsel to Arjun, that dispelled Arjun's doubts upon the battlefield of Kurukshetra! Look at yourself as a spiritual warrior: unlimited and boundless! This will help you become who you are truly born to be!

The infinite power of Divine is always at hand to protect us, guide us, just as Krishna does for Arjun.

When one's path is just, the Infinite does indeed protect us: for example, Krishna shows Arjun how all through the battle of Kurukshetra, it has been Hanuman who has protected Arjun from the enemy's celestial weapons. Hanuman's divine presence has been subtly there with Arjun upon the chariot (he is also on the chariot's flag), and once the battle is won and Arjun alights from his chariot, it bursts into flames! All the while, even without knowing it, Arjun was being protected! So too are we, provided our intentions are right.

Taking Small Steps towards Inner Peace and Power

Small steps go a long way. The Mahabharat illustrates and vividly teaches us that even small initiatives matter: the idea is to keep moving on, letting go, and not holding anything back. It is as the Upanishads say, *"Charaiveti, Charaiveti"* (keep moving forward), an idea that the Buddha also expressed to his disciples much later.

Remember to take a small step every day towards self-realization and greater spiritual knowledge. This brings the inner peace and inner power needed to achieve your potential in all situations. Ultimately, this is the road to enlightened freedom (*mukti, moksha,* or *nirvana*).

Compassion, Empathy, and Spiritual Values

Have compassion *(karuna)* and empathy for all. That allows you to put your own problems in perspective, along with making you realize the value of the shared cosmic journey through time and space that we are all on! Within the Mahabharat, we see how eventually victory is theirs who value spiritual values! Without these values, one cannot realize one's higher nature as a human being. True character arises through kindling your consciousness with these values.

To renounce *ghrina* (contempt)—even for one's enemies—is important. It helps the spiritual warrior have a sense of mystically merciful compassion (*daya*).

In the Indian *Shastras* or holy texts, it is said that duty is all about *compassion before harshness*. It is about *service before self*. It is about *justice before punishment*.

Free Your Mind of All Limitations

Expand your mind. Free your mind. Completely destroy your sense of limitation! Developing an ability to see past all limitations of body-mind, of time and space, is called *aparimita drishti*. We must enhance this within our consciousness.

The Mahabharat is all about teaching us that we are unlimited in our potential for material and spiritual abundance—if only we expand our *chetana* or inner consciousness! Never impose limits on yourself. You are as capable of self-realization and truly empowered living as are the Mahabharat's greatest heroes.

A Meditative Attitude

Finite circumstances and objects will not lead to the ultimate truth: raise your consciousness beyond them every day! That is real meditation. That will allow you to confront and overcome all your fears. It makes your flow of consciousness strong, undisturbed, vast, and empowered. Identify with your innermost soul (*antar-atma*) and the cosmic super-soul (*param-atma*).

Cultivate a meditative attitude: a detached, cool, objective way of viewing life. This is a powerful way of looking at all things. This attitude of *dhyaana* or meditation is at the very root, heart, and soul of the Mahabharat's vast teachings. It creates emotional stillness, mental steadiness, and deep inner silence—allowing you to manifest your life's true spiritual purpose!

Meditation upon ultimate reality or Brahman is called *brahma chintan*, and it is something you must create space for in your life. Besides that, there are numerous other ways to do dhyaana (meditation)—contemplation upon the sacred light within (*jyotir* dhyaana); the meditations of *raja yoga, laya yoga,* and *kundalini yoga; swaroopa* dhyaana (meditation upon one's innately divine nature); *upaasana* or dhyaana upon the *Ishta* (one's chosen deity); as well as various methods of meditation upon the formless or manifest aspect of the Supreme. Always remember this: choose a meditation that you are effortlessly comfortable with! It should come naturally to you, become like your second nature, and percolate through all aspects of your life. Be easy and natural in your meditative attitude: it's essentially about self-internalization and cultivating one's way of looking at things.

CHAPTER - 2

Key Lessons

Human Consciousness

In Indian spirituality and mysticism, it is said that the stronger the roots, the stronger the tree! And our root of being is within our consciousness: strengthen the consciousness and you become stronger in every dimension, material *and* spiritual (in entirety this can be defined as *mind-body-soul*).

The beauty of the Mahabharat is that it contains the deepest insights into human consciousness. And the subject of human consciousness is most important when it comes to dealing with challenges or difficulties in life. When faced with tough times, it is the quality of our consciousness which will determine how we are able to move past them, how we are able to live productively, happily, full of the greatest potential-realization.

Within the Mahabharat, Krishna is the voice of supreme consciousness, helping and guiding our own consciousness to a higher awakened state of spiritual light and successful living. His is the voice of evolution and ascension of consciousness.

On the other hand, blindness and dullness of consciousness is signified by King Dhritarashtra and his son Duryodhan, and it has disastrous consequences. Theirs is the voice of regression and fall of consciousness.

The eternal lesson of the epic is for us to move towards absolutely awakened consciousness or *chaitanya*. This takes us towards our own spiritual liberation or *moksha* as well as makes us more capable of creating well-being within the world (*loka-sangraha*).

The Mahabharat is an incomparable text. At one level it is a story about war, a story about the conflicts between the Pandavs and the Kauravs.

But at another level, it summarizes all human aspirations and feelings, in entirety. It tells us the route towards enlightened living and, most importantly, it tells us how we can find inner peace. In other words, the Mahabharat deals with the momentary material happenings of life as well as the eternal qualities that bring about true quality in living. Ultimately, the Mahabharat teaches us how to rejuvenate all our impulses and actions within the material world through the light of higher consciousness.

Awakening our latent intelligence and cognitive faculties (*chitt-shakti, buddhi-shakti*) is the abiding teaching of the Mahabharat. It is at the heart of Hindu philosophy.

A Guide for Conflict and Resolution

Man's entire story upon earth has been one of conflict. He wages war not only with others but within himself also. It is how to *transcend* the state of conflict and move into a state of bliss that is the guiding secret of the Mahabharat. Eventually, we have to strive towards the higher bliss-state, just as the Pandavs had to on their spiritual quest, long after the events of the war were over.

The Mahabharat is a comprehensive guide. One of the teachings it imparts is having the courage to deal with the various aspects of our relationships based on politics, beliefs, ideologies, religions, so on and so forth. It helps us resolve and better understand our own personal and inter-personal conflicts. Within the Mahabharat are reflected all the significant shades of conflict and conflict-resolution: on the outer sphere, it could be a clash of values or a clash for material gain, but at the level of the inner being it could be a self-conflict or internal crisis (a *dharma-sankat*) as exemplified by Arjun's condition upon the battlefield, before he is rejuvenated by Krishna's divine message of the Bhagvad Gita.

Because the Mahabharat is a very vast text in its many dimensions, the effort in this book has been to condense the most important teachings of this vast scripture, so that it becomes a distilled work that enables us to absorb its most essential life lessons. One such lesson is on how we can attain clarity of vision even amidst uncertainty and an unknown future, clearing the mind of its many doubts and misgivings, its various internal conflicts and sorrows, and emerging full of spiritual light, clarity, strength, courage, and determined resolution.

Wholeness of Being

The whole basis of the Mahabharat is to take us towards wholeness of being, wholeness of happiness in life. How does one achieve this wholeness? By conquering the lesser aspects of being with our uniquely sublime spiritual aspects. It is said in the Mahabharat:

"You must conquer anger through forgiveness. You must conquer the unrighteous by your own righteousness and honesty. You must conquer miserliness by generosity. And you must conquer falsehood by truth."

Akrōdhēna jayētkrōdha-masādhum sādhunā jayēt
jayētkadaryam dānēna jayētsatyēna cānrtam

Living with Authenticity

Authentic understanding, and not just acquired "knowledge", is the most key ability we should manifest in life.

The Mahabharat is a great treasure trove of lessons on how to live your life with authenticity: in a way that you have dropped all illusions and so-called "knowledge" within the mind, and have opened your heart to the greater truth so that you perceive things correctly.

In the Sabha Parva of the Mahabharat, it is said: "When the Divine wants to destroy a person, when the gods want to finish an evil person, they simply destroy his sense of perception. They destroy his mind. That way, he starts seeing things wrongly."

All things in your life will move correctly if you invest yourself in maintaining authentic or correct perception. When your perception is inauthentic, or marred, you automatically move towards destruction. This life lesson can be observed in the Mahabharat through the character of the Kauravs.

So it can be deduced that the Mahabharat talks in metaphors. It is not so much about the gods as it is about our own impulses which determine our lives. It is about our own sense of perceiving, and thereafter *doing*, the right thing, which takes us towards joy, fulfilment, enlightenment, and energetic living.

Living with truthful and authentic perception awakens our latent inner strength, leading to spiritual powers or *siddhis,* such as *vaak-siddhi* (immense power of speech), *prapti* (attainment), *vasitva* (infinite control), etc.

The Non-Egoic State

In the Vana Parva of the Mahabharat, it is said that through gentleness you can defeat the ungentle. In other words, the person without ego is more powerful than the person with ego. And this has been proven time and again through the events of the Mahabharat.

The greatest capacity to take flight into the highest spiritual realization comes from being humble and grounded. So, invest yourself in the non-egotistic approach, for such a state leads to happiness. It is the way to achieve a lightness of being for in this state a person drops all mental burdens, just like a tree sheds its leaves. When you are not shackled by your ego, you become richly imbued with inner clarity, understanding, and dynamism. The great Bheeshma clearly instructs Yudhishthir that while a king is respected by his *praja* or subjects, the person of wisdom is respected by all. And wisdom only begins by dropping ego.

Ego is of many kinds. The *abhimani* (egoist) may have ego about wealth, knowledge, power, the body (*deha-abhimana*), etc. Ultimately, ego is false (*mithya-abhimana*). Passion-driven ego (*rajas-ahamkaar*) and inertia-driven ego (*tama-ahamkaar*) are both damaging. It is good to move towards the state of non-ego (*nir-abhimanata*).

Power

In the Udyoga Parva of the Mahabharat, it is said: "Being intoxicated with power is far worse than being intoxicated with alcohol; because the one who is intoxicated with power does not come to his senses before he collapses and falls." Therefore, never obsess about that which is ultimately non-important: power, name, position!

A major consequence of not subduing the ego (*ahamkara*) is addiction to power or obsession with position. One starts to believe that name, position, or power are all-important. These steadily become a part of one's identity. The Mahabharat, so rich and wide-ranging in its wisdom, shows that neither name nor position nor power are our ultimate reality! Always remember that power and position can be easily taken away at any moment!

From one point of view, the power-struggle and war fought between the Pandavs and the Kauravs appears senseless, for it causes widespread destruction and deaths of many. Even after winning and attaining power, there is no cause for celebration felt by the Pandavs.

It is essential to realize that we are spiritual beings and to focus on the soulfulness of life, which will make us masterful in the spiritual domain, and thereby truly improve the quality of life. Power should not be the aim.

Inner Wisdom

In the Vana Parva of the Mahabharat, it is said: "White hair does not make you a wise being."

Even a child can have wisdom (there are famous examples in Indian tradition such as Ashtavakra, Dhruv, Prahlad, Shuka, and others). It is not about the physical age, nor about the material wealth we have. It is all about cultivating inner wisdom. This idea of inner wisdom is the whole basis of the Mahabharat. If you change something within yourself, everything else in your life changes. Cultivation of inward wisdom, and the change of consciousness within yourself, is the primary teaching of the Mahabharat.

Soulful Poetry

The Mahabharat uses great poetry to express spiritual truths. In that way, it is utterly unique. No other epic in the world, no other poetic work has been able to bring out spiritual truth through metaphors as much as the Mahabharat does. It is a rich repository of powerful poetry compressed in an inimitable way.

For example, look at these lines in the Udyoga Parva of the Mahabharat: "The chariot is our body within which the soul is the driver. Our senses are the horses, and the good driver is undistracted by the horses. He knows how to tame the horses. He keeps them well trained and therefore, the chariot moves smoothly, skilfully."

So beautifully does the author and mystic poet Ved Vyasa illustrate the idea of the human soul. He is telling us something profound: Keep your senses under check, identify yourself with the soul which exists within you. Then the chariot of life will be able to go to destinations that are fulfilling!

Never Be Afraid!

Never be afraid of facing up to things. That is the lesson of Krishna to Arjun in the great scripture the Bhagvad Gita, which forms the very crux or soul of the Mahabharat.

Real victory is a victory of spirit. No matter what is happening on the outside, function as if you are an instrument of this greater existence. With this knowledge, you become fearless and free in mind, body, and soul. You are able to fight your own battles in life just as Arjun did, once the light of Krishna's wisdom dawned within his being.

Fear disallows us from seeing existence and the universe as a great bliss-permeated ocean (*ananda-sagara*). Freeing us from fear is the pith and bulwark of the Mahabharat's mystic message.

Jaya or Victory

The original name of the Mahabharat was *jaya* or victory. It is evident then that the way to be "victorious" was a crucial tenet in the creation of the text. While the epic has lessons on how to achieve victory in the material sphere of our life, its core lessons are about how *real victory* in life is in the spiritual sphere. The Mahabharat teaches us to never get cowed down by how invincible the enemy is or how insurmountable the circumstances may seem! Come on to the "battlefield" of life with boldness! Realize that human life is limited, but it is our *quality of consciousness* that determines our success or victory. Through realizing this, you are able to meet all life challenges in a manner which is truly worthy of that divinity which dwells within you!

The Mahabharat is about victory or jaya in war, but it is also about how to achieve peace of mind, of heart, and of the soul!

Shaanti or Peace: The Yogic Essence

The Mahabharat is all about going from *ashaanti* (mental unrest) to *parama-shaanti* (ultimate peace).

In order to be at your best, you must always remain calm and peaceful. Shaanti or peacefulness imbues us with calm courage and leads to true liberation and enlightenment. In your day-to-day life, your ability to deal with things undergoes a transformation once you make peace within yourself.

Coming into a peaceful *union* with the Divine which exists within you (which is *yoga* in essence), is both the goal *and* the means which the Mahabharat tells us to act with. It imparts us with yogic values: drop the bondages of anger, flow in a manner which is full of wisdom and peaceful wonder. If need be, we are to drop the bondages of shallow social "morality" even, and invest our energies towards higher realization!

The point is this: do whatever you have to do in life with peaceful serenity. Then even the act of war can turn into an act of meditation, just as Arjun demonstrates on the instructions of Krishna!

A Divine Cosmic Matrix

The Mahabharat teaches us that we exist within a divine cosmic matrix and are connected to each glorious aspect of it. What is there to be scared of when the Divine is always beside you, guiding you? Once you are aware of your inborn relationship with the Divine, you flow relaxed and strong upon the river of life. You effortlessly and actively do all that you need to do, with grace and vigour! And yet you remain a pure witness to everything, filled with calm inner silence.

Knowing that the power of the divine matrix resides within you—along with the timelessly creative universal energy—takes you to a feeling of vastness and infiniteness! This attitude of feeling oneness with the divine leads to *nitya-sukha:* eternal happiness. This idea is at the heart of the Mahabharat's most profound spiritual teachings (contained within the numerous sacred dialogues or "gitas" within it, including the Bhagvad Gita, Sampaka Gita, Anu Gita, Uttara Gita, Vichakhnu Gita, Vritra Gita, and Manki Gita).

Harmony

Deep within your being, create harmony. By studying the various "gitas" embedded within the Mahabharat (including the Uttara Gita and Parashar Gita), we realize that creation of inner and outer harmony/equilibrium (*samyavastha*) is a key spiritual lesson.

There are four steps to mental and spiritual harmony:

The first step is to cultivate simplicity. Simplicity of being leads to spiritual and mental harmony.

The second step is to not create disharmony within yourself by *identification or attachment with the senses*. Often in the Mahabharat, our being is likened to a "chariot", which we must steer in the right way. It signifies our being in totality. Attachment with the senses will only make the "chariot" of one's being go helter-skelter! You don't want each "horse" (or sense) to run in its own direction, on its own whims and fancies! It must run in harmony with the other horses, thereby taking the "chariot" to the correct destination.

The third step is with reference to a saying in the Udyoga Parva of the Mahabharat: "Never do to other people that which is obnoxious to you. Always do that which is pleasing, which you'd like done to yourself." This is a golden rule! Never treat others the way you would not like to be treated. This is the secret of lighting the spiritual lamp within your being. It is the secret to attaining true self-respect and respect for others. It enlightens your consciousness. It brings a feeling of compassion (karuna), and energy (shakti). When this is done, you begin to feel harmonious within your being and become connected to a higher source. This helps you move in harmony with people, and with all things. It enables you to function with a silent lightness of being, a freedom of being. Not clinging to things, you begin to have gratitude for your life and courage to accept any difficulty (even death) with grace. These aspects are the very pillars of spiritual radiance.

The fourth step is to remember that change is inherent in existence. Just like the seasons change, circumstances in life change! Accept change and thereby attain inward harmony! The Mahabharat is all about acceptance of change. Only they who can adapt to change eventually emerge victorious. This is a key lesson for dealing with problems in life. It is change that triggers evolution within human consciousness. Changes lead to adjustment in human society: at the terrestrial level, at the level of ideas, politics, economics, environment, and so on.

The fifth step to cultivate harmony is to know that all true victory is within your own state of energy and consciousness. It is within the quality of energy or *prana* which you have. This holds the key to winning, to victory, to conquering all circumstances that may seem adverse. Correct your state of energy and consciousness, and you move into the highest realm of spirituality! It is also important, from the Mahabharat's point of view, to understand that we don't *know it all:* there are layers and layers to reality. What we think of as spirituality may not be actually in consonance with true mysticism. Be alert to the truth of things. And with this humility of being, you are able to face life with an openness of mind. Identify with and manifest your highest energy and latent power of consciousness, because the moment you identify with the base things, you are off the spiritual path, and in disharmony.

Playfulness or Leela

In the Hindu view of life, all things come out of a divine Leela or playfulness. Be playful, no matter what circumstances you are facing. Life is a game! Stay grounded, don't get carried away by fear, and don't get carried away by overconfidence either. Being grounded gives you the ability to be courageous in the face of all things. Leela implies both a playful and a loving attitude in life.

Within the Mahabharat, Krishna exemplifies the idea of Leela or divine playfulness. In the system of the *Dasha* Avatars or divine manifestations of Lord Vishnu, each avatar is said to have his own divine play upon earth. Yet Krishna stands apart because of his completely effortless, playful attitude.

Playfulness begets its own courage: it makes us shed the mental and emotional baggage of conditioned fears. Eventually, spiritual courage is the very essence not only of the Mahabharat but of all Indian spiritual texts. Fear nothing! The earth is a stage upon which we are all enacting a play. Enact your part calmly. This will make you spontaneous, and you will be effortless and non-tense in your actions.

Spontaneity

The lessons of the Mahabharat are to be imbibed and listened to deeply. Yet eventually, it is *your inner state of spontaneous being* which is most important. Spontaneity cannot be bought. No riches can buy the spiritual wealth of the effortless, spontaneous, and free state of inner being i.e. the state of the rishi, the seer, the sage!

Learn to live as free energy, one which knows bliss to be that which is *beyond* what happens to the body or the physical state of being. Never fear what will happen to you tomorrow. Krishna tells Arjun: "*Na hanyate hanyamane sarire,*" implying that nothing can eventually destroy you, nothing can ultimately harm you from the spiritual point of view. Even if the body is destroyed, your soul can find spiritual bliss. Your ultimate happiness of being is *beyond all physical or material happenings: it exists as your self-nature.* Look at material events like you would at the changing patterns of the sky. Within the sky, clouds come and go. But behind that changing cloud-cover is the unchanging greater reality, which, from the mystical point of view, is the Ultimate Reality. Identify with that Ultimate Reality. That releases the great power of spontaneity that is latent within you.

Inner Richness

The greatest gift of the Mahabharat is its lesson of inner richness. This implies inner prayer, inner freedom, inner compassion, inner awareness, and ultimately, an inner state of ease. These qualities allow us to happily accept life as a divine drama—unfolding a new act every day. Through such an attitude and state of being, you are able to meet all difficult circumstances in life with courage, truth, and higher consciousness!

Important Aspects

There are many other poignant aspects that the Mahabharat illustrates.

It talks of the highest values which the Indian civilization has stood for. The battle of Kurukshetra, which is in a way the centrepiece of the Mahabharat, is a battle for righteousness. On one side are the Pandavs: Yudhishthir, Bheem, Arjun, Nakul and Sahadev—all mighty warriors, all peerlessly wise in their own ways. And on their side comes Krishna, the enigmatic, mysterious symbol of cosmic vastness. On the other side are arrayed Duryodhan and his brothers, the Kauravs, who are fighting to defend the indefensible. Now, both sides are facing a crisis. But it is the side of the Pandavs—which faces crisis with nobility and justice in their hearts—that eventually triumphs. The lesson being this: never fail to have the courage to stand up for what is right! That is the first thing: have integrity of being, have an aspiration for truth of being. These ultimately triumph! The old adage in India is *Satyameva Jayate*: "Truth always triumphs." If you stand for right consciousness and truth, your life will automatically move towards happiness.

To make peace within yourself, to find joy and blissful realization within yourself at both psychological and spiritual levels, always remember to seek the Sat-Chit-Ananda of being: truth, then higher consciousness, and then bliss or Ananda comes automatically!

The Mahabharat is most interesting because it tells us something very intriguing: that man is a very baffling mix of contradictions! Man is capable of deep compassion, but also of deep jealousy. He is capable of the highest love and of the deepest hate! He is capable of the greatest insight and of blind ignorance.

Hatred and envy is signified by the character of Duryodhan. His father, King Dhritarashtra signifies literal and psychological blindness. The aspect of spiritual grace and surrender is missing from their lives. Hence, when faced with crisis, they crumble and fall.

The Mahabharat is in this way an echo of all that humanity is. It is also an echo of that infinite energy which lies beyond humanity, and to whom life and death are mere bubbles upon the ocean of the cosmos (*brahmanda, vishwa*). When we look at things in this vaster light, which the Mahabharat encourages us to do, we understand that we are to go beyond our self-importance, we are to go beyond our ideas of victory and defeat.

CHAPTER - 3

Krishna and the Bhagvad Gita

At the heart and soul of the Mahabharat is the Bhagvad Gita. The Bhagvad Gita (the divine song) of Krishna condenses this vast epic's most important teachings and contains the very essence of India's great ancient scriptures—the Upanishads. For this reason, it is also referred to as the *Gitopanishad*.

The biggest differentiator between Krishna and all other mystics of the world remains this: he can be effortlessly playful about the most profound topics, and effortlessly bridge both the mystical and material aspects of existence. This takes him beyond all categories, definitions, or boundaries. His Bhagvad Gita stands for complete freedom from all bondages, leading us to ultimate dynamism and excellence!

The setting of the Gita is unique: Arjun stands on the battlefield of Kurukshetra, riddled with inner turmoil and ready to drop his weapons. He has rooted family bonds with the enemy, the Kauravs—they are his kinsmen, after all. He has cousins, uncles, teachers, gurus, friends, against whom he has to fight! And being the great warrior he is, he has to ultimately kill them! He is questioning this destruction. Krishna, Arjun's divine charioteer in the war, then delivers a spiritual discourse. The guidance provided to Arjun has a universal quality, and contains the highest counsel to all human beings—who often have to deal with harsh circumstances in life.

In a way, the essence of the *entire* Mahabharat is captured by the mystical persona of Krishna: as a spiritual guide, the paragon of dynamism, the most multi-faceted being, and the godhead. His is the eternal voice of wisdom, which is at the centre of

Indian civilization. It is for that reason that Krishna is called Yogeshwara: the Lord of Yoga, the master who teaches us the essence of spiritual wisdom.

Karma Yoga: Right Action

A key lesson we must glean from the Bhagvad Gita is that of Karma Yoga or the mystical philosophy of right action and work. The main point of Karma Yoga is to be *emotionally and mentally detached from one's actions,* and instead cultivate mystical consciousness within ourselves. We must become pure witnesses of our own actions (*karma-saakshi*), instead of being attached to the fruit of our actions.

Krishna tells Arjun: *"Arjun, you are not entitled to the fruit of your action. You are only entitled to the action itself. Therefore, never act for the fruits of action. Do not be attached to actions. But at the same time, do not be attached to inaction or non-action . . . Be in* samadhi, *be of steady intellect, for that is yoga . . . Do not give in to the impotence and fear of the mind. That is not our true nature. Give up weakness and arise . . . Don't grieve for those who you shouldn't grieve for. The soul experiences all stages of life: childhood, youth, old age. Do not be deluded by these changes . . . The soul keeps on taking fresh clothes and finding a new body. The soul cannot be cut by a sword, it cannot be burnt by fire, it cannot become wet by water. It is eternal, endless, non-changing. So, do not grieve . . . Do not invest your mind in the objects of the senses."*

In other words, we can see the essence of spirituality in Krishna's words. He goes on in the chapter on Karma Yoga to tell Arjun:

"It is not through action or renunciation that you become perfect. Every being has to act. That is the way of nature . . . Even for me, Arjun, for whom there is no duty in the entire cosmos, I am constantly at work . . . Each person thinks they are the doer. That is an illusion, a delusion . . . Do your duty well in your own self-nature. It's better to die in that self-nature than to act in another's nature."

Here we can see Krishna expounding the essence of Karma Yoga to free Arjun from his fears, so that he can act as a warrior upon the battlefield. In totality, we are to cultivate a carefree yet dynamic attitude, not worrying about results but carrying on in selfless work.

Gyaana Yoga: Right Knowledge

Gyaana Yoga is the pure path of wisdom and right knowledge. In chapter four of the Gita on Gyaana Yoga, Krishna tells Arjun: *"Destroy all doubt through the sword of wisdom. Be harmonious within yourself. Be in a state of yoga, and arise to do your part . . . I manifest when unrighteousness goes beyond limits. I am born from age to age for creating good, for destroying the evil, for exalting the righteous . . . Whatever way you want to reach me, whatever path you take, you will come to me in the end . . . Within action, be in inaction, and within inaction, be in action. That is wisdom. That is the heart of the Yogi. Create self-harmony within yourself."*

In chapter five, Arjun asks Krishna what is preferable between action and the renunciation of action. Krishna advises him:

"Action is preferable to renunciation . . . Be non-affected by karma. Put your mind to Yoga . . . Purify your mind, subdue the senses. Thereby, even in your action, you remain non-affected by karma . . . A true sage is one who can see all things as equal . . . The person of wisdom does not seek to find happiness in external objects. Those only create unhappiness."

Further, Krishna says: *"The person who sees me everywhere and sees all things as part of me does not ever lose me."*

So here again, we can see Krishna creating this sense of spiritual openness within Arjun, taking him away from the imprisonment of thoughts, taking him away from the agony that he has created in his mind, and taking him towards understanding the totality of being.

Raja Yoga: Steadiness of Mind

Raja Yoga is the "royal" path of meditativeness in all things, and amidst all circumstances. In the Mahabharat, the spiritual aim of Krishna is to make Arjun's mind steady.

Arjun says: *"The mind is so unsteady. It's easier to control the wind than the mind."*

But Krishna reassures him that there is a spiritual solution to this conundrum of the mind. He says:

"Arjun, without a doubt, the mind is fickle; but through practice and non-attachment, it can be overcome . . . The greatest being is the Yogi. Therefore, be a Yogi, Arjun."

Through true yoga, one moves towards the bliss of meditation, spiritual understanding, and perfection. As Krishna teaches, it is all about our striving for that enlightened state.

Krishna says: *"Out of thousands of people, only a few strive for perfection, and out of those few, perhaps only one would know my truth."*

He then speaks of his maya, which causes people to be deluded, saying:

"I am hidden by Yogmaya. The world does not truly know me as being immortal. My divine illusion is hard to pierce. Whilst I know all my past and future existences, no one quite knows me."

In other words, it is difficult to know absolute reality, the godhead. But through meditatively mystic insight, spiritual learning, through sadhana or spiritual discipline, we are able to reach that godhead. And the beauty is that the Divine remains hidden deep within our heart as a song, as a dance, as a fragrance. The means to attain the Divine are prescribed in the Bhagvad Gita.

While expounding the system of Raja Yoga, Krishna says that he is completely unattached, neutral. Yet he is concerned for the welfare of all. If only we have an undistracted mind and unite ourselves with the divine spirit, do we move towards enlightened being and fearless living.

Bhakti Yoga: Pure Devotion

Bhakti Yoga is the yoga of devotion. The essence of it is to cultivate a deeply devotional relationship with the Divine. It is about uniting with the Supreme through pure love (prema).

Krishna represents the absolute reality. He says:

"As one age ends, all beings come into me. And going inward again and again, I create the whole multitude of beings. All are dependant within my nature . . . The cosmos revolves accordingly . . . Most don't know me as the great lord. But those who worship me with a non-distracted being are able to unite themselves with me in the state of yoga . . . Even a sinner, if he worships me with the might of his soul or Atma, is able to reach me . . . He who loves me reaches peace, tranquillity. I am Vasudeva, I am Vyasa, I am also the poet Ushana . . . True devotees serve me, see me as time, and time takes all to their end. It is the ancient slayer . . ."

Krishna is teaching Arjun to create a relationship with the supremely divine aspect that he, Krishna, is. So far, Arjun had related to Krishna as a friend and as a brother-in-law. But the whole task before Arjun, and indeed before us all, is to link ourselves with that divine reality which Krishna represents.

The Secret

Krishna's effort is to take Arjun beyond the boundaries of so-called rational thought, which is often limited in intuitivity. To understand the dimensions of the soul, of the divine, what we consider to be our perfectly logical minds are often found wanting. Spiritual knowledge is gleaned through intuitivity, and that is what Krishna guides Arjun towards.

Arjun asks Krishna very specifically to take him towards knowing the intuitive secret of the true *Atman* or soul that exists within. Upon Arjun's request, Krishna shows himself in his *Virat Roop* or the great cosmic form. Doing so, he says:

"Arjun, behold my glorious, unending, imperishable form—within which the gods, the Rudras, the Ashwins, the Vasus, the Adityas, the Maruts exist."

All things in creation—whether inanimate or animate—come before Arjun's eyes, like a flash of lightning. Through the divine vision Krishna has enabled him to have, he is able to see the unending glory which the universal form of Krishna represents! And that universal form is described as wondrous, limitless, as if thousands of suns are blazing. As if the entire universe, indeed many universes, exist within the being of Krishna!

Arjun becomes filled with wonder. He bows to the Lord with folded hands and he begs for mercy. He says: *"Lord, why are you in this very fierce form? My salutations to you!"*

Krishna then instructs Arjun: *"You see me as time or Kaal, Arjun, that which destroys all things."* He tells Arjun to not grieve, to not think that he—Arjun—is about to destroy his enemies. Arjun is to see that *he is only an instrument* of Krishna. All shall be as Krishna wills! Arjun realizes he is only a tool of Krishna's divine intent.

Krishna asserts himself as being the only destroyer, the one who causes everything to come to non-existence. Krishna says, *"I am time, I am Kaal itself, and I manifest to destroy all worlds. Arjun, my form is very difficult to see. You are fortunate that you have seen me, because not even the greatest beings have seen my full form. If you fix your mind upon my glorious, divine form, you will become affixed in knowing that undefinable form of mine through which all beings come to me."*

Krishna advises Arjun to rest all his knowledge and understanding within him. To not *do* anything as such apart from fixing his consciousness upon

Krishna, through yoga. And to know that Krishna *does* all the actions! Knowing this, Krishna says, Arjun would attain perfection. Arjun is to renounce the fruit of action and thereby feel peaceful.

Arjun is to be friendly, kind to all creatures, and to get rid of the egoic eye as propounded by Krishna. Yet he is to be the complete warrior he is! Being so, Arjun would attain yoga, and become fixed with determination, established in *viveka* or discrimination. So doing, Arjun would not become disturbed by the activities of the world. So doing, he would become even dearer to Krishna.

Arjun comes to know, through Krishna, that true wisdom is always superior to so-called yogic practice. Krishna explains it in many ways. That the state of meditation is more worthy than the state of just knowledge. That Arjun is to renounce his attachment to actions, and then realize the state of meditation that is followed by supreme peacefulness. Arjun is to be free of expectations, be unconcerned by circumstances, be totally carefree and dynamic. And then, he will have neither so-called *happiness* nor so-called *sorrow*: he will go beyond these, towards supreme blissfulness and assimilation into the divine being! He will become tranquil. He (Arjun) will become of a calm disposition because he would have renounced all attachment. And such a person is indeed very dear to him, says Krishna.

Krishna teaches Arjun that the body is the *kshetra* or the field. Within this field is true knowledge. If you know this field to be manifest with the soul, you will know the supreme, the unending. You will move towards the state of *Sattva*. You will move beyond the state of *Rajas* and *Tamas*, which take you downward. All action is by the *gunas*, says Krishna. Beyond the gunas or elements of nature, does Krishna exist. Knowing this, we can attain union or yoga with Krishna.

Krishna says:

"I am indeed the source of all wisdom. I am indeed the source of the Vedas, the end of the Vedanta. I am like the Ashvattha *tree whose roots are in the divine, and its branches move towards the earth. Within each of its leaves is the Veda. I am within you as I am within the heart of all beings. I am the very source of wisdom. I am the origin of Vedic knowledge and Vedanta. I am the non-destructible, the supreme being, the imperishable. I am beyond the soul also, the* Jivatma, *and thereby I am known as the* Purushottam, *the ultimate. I cast into delusion those that don't understand me. Remember, you must renounce anger, greed, lust. These are the gateways*

to hell. Worship the great, worship those who shine with spiritual knowledge . . . Come to me, I will give you the ultimate liberation."

Dissolving All Delusions

Arjun responds by saying that all his delusions are completely dismissed, his doubts are completely gone! He has heard from Yogeshwara, the lord of yoga himself, and thereby he moves towards a state which is beyond renunciation and beyond action.

Krishna advises Arjun to not forsake his duties, to be worship-ful, to do that which is propounded in the Vedic rituals, yet never give in to conceit and never think that he is apart from the divine *because the lord exists within the very heart and soul of all beings!*

Knowing so, Arjun can attain ultimate peace. Knowing so, he can attain ultimate divine refuge. Knowing so, he can move towards the spirit of true service. Knowing so, he can attain the knowledge of the deepest mystery that Krishna represents!

It is about awakening from wrong notions (*bhram, bhraanti*), and going towards non-attachment and non-delusion (the *nirmoha* state).

Lessons from the Bhagvad Gita

The greatness of the Bhagvad Gita is unparalleled. It is not only the ultimate text on *adhyatma-vidya* (spiritual knowledge), but also on *chitta-vidya* (being a scientific exposition on the mind and on psychology).

The Mahabharat is, in a way, condensed in entirety within the seven hundred verses of the Bhagvad Gita. There are several key lessons the Gita offers for tackling life's challenges, circumstances, and tough times:

1. All three aspects of life—the psychological and emotional, the physical, and the spiritual—need to be in a certain unity or yoga of being. Then only can we become dynamic in what we do. Without a unity of mind, body, and soul, we remain weak: we remain people who are not able to act with any source of inner integrity and strength. Just like Arjun finds solace in the message of mind-body-spirit unity or yoga that Krishna is talking about, so too we must pay attention to all three aspects in our lives. Paying attention

itself creates a great strength of help from the universe, from the divine element, from the greater energy from which we all come. Help is always at hand! That is Krishna's abiding lesson to Arjun. Like Arjun, all we need to do is make our plea and surrender ourselves to the message of the Greater, thereby becoming refreshed at all three levels of our being! Through such surrender comes synthesis, soulfulness, and serenity.

2. You should never feel that you are small, that you are helpless and weak. Arjun is feeling very weak, very helpless! A warrior of his stature is down on his knees, completely depleted of all energy, of all strength. The whole idea of Krishna is that we are to understand we are part of a great immensity of life. Never lose self-respect, never lose that feeling that the Divine is with you! Krishna reassures Arjun that he exists within him also (thereby lifting him up from the state of feeling weak, without self-power). So the infinite power is always with you! This is very important to remember, especially when facing a difficult situation in life.

3. The only way to come out of the morass of difficult situations is to first of all drop your fears: to become courageous! This is a decision you have to make. Start by dropping your fears. If you can do that, then you are able to take the first step into moving from the darkness towards the light. All great journeys in life begin with having the courage to walk the path. You simply take the first step fearlessly, and then life itself makes you walk on ahead. Always have the courage to take that first step boldly, in all things. Krishna bestows Arjun *abhaya-dana*: the ultimate gift of non-fear, courage!

4. For new spiritual wisdom to dawn, we are to completely forget all our pre-conditioned thought processes. Leave all those! Open up your heart and mind to the fresh spiritual nourishment of the Greater. That is your ultimate nourishment. Eventually, all of our conditioned thoughts cannot help us understand our ultimate reality and mystic vastness! What *can* help us is an awakening into our greater spiritual reality, because with that we come into a state of being

where we can reach God-consciousness or Krishna-consciousness. And that is what eventually makes you live and act in a meditative manner, in a manner that is meaningful, in a manner that strengthens you at the level of intellect, feelings, action, and most importantly, at the level of your spiritual being.

5. You are to know that you are made up of the abiding Ananda or bliss element. Eventually, the entire universe, all of creation is comprised of bliss. Ananda is the most abiding spiritual aspect of Indian civilization. In fact, in the formula Sat-Chit-Ananda, you will find that life is a movement from Sat or truth, to consciousness or Chitta, to bliss which is Ananda. Knowing your capacity for Ananda is very important for you to open your being to a larger potential, which is what Arjun does eventually by standing up to fight on the battlefield of Kurukshetra.

6. We are to first give up the fight which we are having internally. Arjun is in self-conflict, he is in self-doubt. And through inner conflict what happens is that you become weakened.

Within yourself, have the energy to emerge victorious, have the energy to say to yourself, "No matter what, I will be able to transcend all my negative feelings, all my negative thoughts, all my negative circumstances!" Through this thought, you are able to emerge evolved, just as from the caterpillar emerges the butterfly. The process of chrysalis, transformation, or change happens with this essential learning. We are to eventually drop spiritual doubtfulness (*asam-bhavana*) and imagined mentation (*vikalpa*), and move towards the state of sheer determination and conviction (*nischaya*)!

7. The vibe you must create within yourself has to be one of radiant energy. Life is all about the level of energy that you're feeling. Vibrating with radiance of good energy is key in the face of tough times. People who vibrate with a radiance of being or joy of being, are always natural leaders. Arjun, in the midst of his despondency, has lost his natural radiance! Hearing Krishna's words, he regains it and is able to *fight the fight* as he must. And remember, his fight is one for justice. Hence,

it is immensely important for him to feel this radiance of being by dropping all guilt.

8. Life is multi-dimensional. Never get caught up in a one-dimensional view of life. Arjun has taken a very narrow, uni-dimensional view of life. He is insisting that things are bleak. He is insisting that life is meaningless. It is when we drop this uni-dimensional way of looking at life that we are able to appreciate the larger aspects of it. Free your mind! Eventually, that is what Arjun does. And he is able to see the universe, the cosmos, the divine, and all of human existence as a play of multi-dimensional forces. So doing, he performs his duty, he does his karma as a warrior, as he's meant to. This is a very key secret to fight any sort of battle in our life. Eventually, the Bhagvad Gita is about fighting your battles in the best state of inward energy. If you can do that, you are already on the path to greater success.

9. Within the innermost core of your being lies the ability of joy. Joy and true happiness does not come from the outside. Joy and true happiness come from your innermost core.

We are capable of ultimate joy inwardly: *brahma-ananda*! Hence, do what you have to do in the world; but to understand true happiness in life, always *internalize*. Arjun is made to *internalize* by Krishna. Arjun's whole focus is on the enemy. Suddenly, Krishna turns the spotlight back into Arjun's interior-most being! And having that spotlight within his being, Arjun is able to evolve from that inward space, that space of consciousness within. Remember this: *internalize to evolve*.

10. We must be wholehearted and total in our action. Arjun is behaving in a manner which is very vacillating, unsure, indecisive. This indecisiveness has made him very weak in the face of the battle. Krishna is telling him to let go of his inhibitions, to let go of all that is holding him back, and thereby respond as he is meant to, to the challenge which is facing him. And that is the way we must respond to all challenges facing us. Never shirk! Always realize that beyond the physical fact and the mental fact of being frightened by any situation, you are supported by the

immensity of the infinite and immeasureable (the *ananta* and *amaatra* divine dimension of existence).

11. Never be apprehensive of fear, as fear is a natural phenomenon. Now, Arjun is a great warrior: he hardly ever feels fear. He is a master of martial science (*kshatriya-vidya*) and the warrior's code (*kshatradharma*). And that is why he is extremely disturbed on the battlefield of Kurukshetra, because for the first time perhaps, a dread has gripped him that is making him unable to fight. But the root of his fear is not the fear of injury or death as such. It is the fear of inflicting wrong. It is the fear of inflicting injuries and death wrongfully upon people. His fear comes from guilt! You have to drop all guilt. You have to act according to the best you can, no matter what.

Do not get psychologically fearful. It is psychological and emotional fear which blinds us, which makes us behave like the proverbial deer caught in the headlights: unable to act, paralyzed! This is what happens to most people in difficult circumstances.

When they have to make great decisions, they freeze, become mentally paralyzed. That is why it is important to understand the spiritual message of the Gita. Sometimes, you have to ignore your own thoughts and feelings. Then only do you attain a greater clarity, a greater vision in life. Being obsessed with thoughts and feelings has often been the greatest downfall of human beings. Much of man's injustices in the world have been based upon thoughts and feelings of hatred, jealousy, fear of the other, etc. The true warrior has no place for all that. He or she is willing to play their unique part in the battlefield of life in whatever way he or she has to: even if that means negating thoughts, negating debilitating emotions.

12. Always remember that the power and strength of the Divine come through *love (prema-bhava)*. The more lovingly devoted you are to the Divine, and the more wonder and awe you have for the universal power, the greater the strength that will fill you. That is why it is said that spiritual strength is the greatest strength. Up until the Gita episode,

Arjun has relied on his own strength, his own ability as a warrior. But when he breaks down on the battlefield of Kurukshetra is when Krishna imbues him with spiritual strength! This idea to keep *spiritual strength* as the very source of our *inner strength*, is the whole basis of the Bhagvad Gita. It takes you towards inner realization, towards inner meditativeness, and creates that dynamic change within you which is needed for the toughest situations in life. *Aantarik-prema*, or totality of love, is the key!

13. Be intense and total in whatever you do, but always remember that you must have a little bit of detachment (*anasakti or vairagya*). The idea of detachment is very key in the Bhagvad Gita and in all scriptures, not only in India but around the world. This is so especially in the Sanatan Dharma of India: you can look at the message of the Vedas, the Upanishads, the Vedanta, and so on. Within these you'd find that the idea of being detached makes you liberated in mind, body, and soul. And then only are you able to act with deep determination, and with all

the power available to you. Else, you become unable to meet your full potential and unable to act with your innermost dynamic ability.

14. You are to move in a natural harmony with the universal energy, the divine energy. Krishna represents the highest energy within the universe and beyond the universe. Arjun has created a situation where he has moved away from this nourishing energy of the divine. He has become too involved and self-conscious within his own mind, his own heart. He has cut himself off from the natural flow of dynamism, which is the very stuff of the cosmos. The whole cosmos—all of creation—is dynamic. All of life is a dynamic flow of energy! We must align ourselves and come into an inner harmony, an inner unity with this energy. That gives us the strength to transcend all difficult times in life.

15. Never fear the unknown. Death is the greatest unknown: Arjun is caught in a dilemma because he is very ignorant about what death actually means. All his life he has been a warrior, he has had to kill enemies, he has had to face difficulties and move past all

guilt in hurting others on the field of battle. Yet, his knowledge of the spiritual reality of death is insufficient. He trembles at the idea of the death of his own kinsmen, his loved ones. He had no problem killing people he didn't know. But when it comes to killing people whom he knows and whom he has loved and respected, he is in a great dilemma.

Krishna's Bhagvad Gita is eventually a dialogue about death itself. Krishna explains to Arjun that life and death are joined in one constant cycle. Death is not the end of existence. Death is but another horizon. When you understand this spiritual idea about death, you are able to transcend all fear of it.

It is very important in human life to address the idea of death. Never fear the inevitable. In fact, the great mystic Swami Vivekananda used to teach to never fear what will happen in the future, to never fear what will happen tomorrow. Death comes to all! Never fear its psychological and emotional disturbances. Be ready to face it yourself, and be ready to understand the greater spiritual dimensions of it. That way, you move towards true mystical and spiritual understanding, and are able to face up to even the most dire situations in life in a wise manner.

16. It is good to achieve things in the world, yet in achieving those do not become anxious. We live in a material world: there are so many things we want to achieve. But in the very achievement of those things we often get into anxiousness, we get into mental turmoil and sadness (*vishaada*). It creates all sorts of psychological and emotional problems for us, which is why over-achievers often lead very frustrated and unhappy personal lives. Very few are those people who act effortlessly even while *achieving* things. And that is the state of being that Krishna is trying to bring Arjun into. Act with dynamism, but act with effortlessness! Don't keep any anxiety in your being. This is key to understand when faced with difficult circumstances in life. It frees you up to act in a manner that expresses the highest within you.

17. Never be afraid to be vulnerable. It is often in vulnerable moments—or what we often call

"weak" moments—that transformational awakening (*prabuddha*) happens! This is why Arjun is able to become transformed on the battlefield of Kurukshetra. It is at Arjun's weakest moment that the Divine has come to rescue him and teach him. So never feel guilty about feeling weak. Every human being, no matter how strong (even the greatest warrior Arjun) suffers weakness. Never shirk from that.

We live in a world where weakness is considered, somehow, not a good thing. But sometimes, it is only when we break down completely that we can emerge afresh. It's like in Egyptian tradition: the phoenix arising from the ashes!

Arjun has gone into a heap of ashes: he is utterly destroyed within, broken. But then only does he remake himself! Then only does he get the blessing and the divine wisdom of Krishna. And he is able to rise up, stand, and fight. So must we all look at difficult circumstances in life in the same manner. You can cry, you can weep, you can go into a situation where you feel that things have come to an end. But always remember, there is light at the end of the tunnel. Through that darkness, you can emerge into the light.

18. Often, those things we think to be burdens actually give us the wings to fly to greater heights. Arjun is thinking he's been burdened with the responsibility of war, of leading the Pandav army against the Kauravs, which is a duty he doesn't want to do. But it is only through taking the responsibility that he emerges as a greater spiritual soul, and he is able to go higher into the sky of spiritual realization. Hence, take on the responsibility, however much you can. This is a teaching echoed again and again by Swami Vivekananda. Always remember, the greatest leaders, the spontaneous leaders in life are those who never reject responsibility. Rather, they take it on, no matter what the circumstance is. That allows you to evolve. That allows you to transcend tough times.

19. Nothing is more valuable than the spiritual vision of inner victory—the victory of one's life-energy (*praana-jaya*). All the riches of the world, all the victories within the world

pale in significance before the inner victory. And Krishna is trying to create that sense of inner victory within Arjun. Yes, he does remind him of his material responsibility: he calls him by his several names, for example, Dhananjaya—the winner of wealth. Arjun has always been one who has won material victories for his side: conquered territory, gathered riches. But ultimately, the greatest wealth, the greatest diamond, is *within* Arjun. It is within the domain of his consciousness. And it is that domain of consciousness that Krishna is opening Arjun's eyes to, so that he can see that this consciousness within him is the most worthy, the most blissful. Becoming aware of his own being, Arjun is able to fight and move beyond the situation that he has been presented with, with heroism, courage/bravery. And by following Krishna's teachings, Arjun sets a good example for all.

20. You are as much a part of god or the Divine (Ishvara) as it is part of you. Never think that you are isolated from the Divine. The Divine is always at hand, close by. It dwells within you, infinitely. Knowing this infiniteness of

yourself is knowing that you are not alone, you are not abandoned, you are cared for!

In our moments of crisis, we often feel that we are alone. We feel abandoned by friends, we feel abandoned by those we love. And this creates fear within us. The enduring lesson of the Bhagvad Gita is that when you truly need help, such divine grace is available to you as you could have never imagined. Knowing this is true faith!

21. One of the greatest things about the personality of Arjun is that he's very sincere, a person of immense *sadgun* (virtuous qualities). That is why Krishna has actually picked him out to be with during the battle of Kurukshetra, and why he's chosen to be Arjun's charioteer! It is all building up towards this playful situation of the Divine, where he is able to be with Arjun during the moment of emotional and mental crisis. So when Arjun breaks down upon the chariot and expresses whatever he has to, from the core of his heart, it is directly to the Divine. And this quality of sincerity marks Arjun out. He is not a hypocrite. He doesn't pretend

to be a moralist. On the other hand, he is genuinely concerned about harming others whom he is fond of, whom he loves. This very sincerity is the greatest spiritual asset for a person who is facing a crisis of any sort, because when you're sincere, the Infinite is always with you. The power of the greater will never abandon the truly sincere seeker, the truly sincere person.

22. We must understand the vastness (*brihattva*) of this human life and cosmic existence.

Before his dialogue with Krishna, Arjun has a certain limitation in his worldview: he's not able to appreciate the vastness of all things. Krishna reveals the vastness and glory of the cosmos, and more importantly, of that godhead he represents as the very progenitor of the cosmos. Looking at things in such a vast light allows us to not get caught up in the problems of the small self, and instead allows us to appreciate things in a broader manner. And when we do that, we become better equipped to deal with circumstances. We are then able to deal with things with a certain calmness of being.

23. Life is full of contradictions. Life and death, day and night, the changing seasons: all opposites move in a cycle. Hence, we have to be ready for change. This is the very idea that Krishna is trying to instil into Arjun. Arjun has taken life to be as he's always known it to be. But *the inflection point* happens on the battlefield of Kurukshetra. And Krishna is telling him how change is in the very nature of existence. Understanding it, and adapting to such change, determines our ability to face up to all crisis moments and difficult situations in life. It creates a flame of vital spirituality (*gyaana-agni*) within us.

24. *Each moment* is an opportunity to become enlightened. Even the battlefield is a fit place, and wartime a fit time, to become enlightened! This is a key lesson of the Gita.

   The moment just before going into conflict can in fact be the most transformational moment. This is one of the most interesting things about the whole episode of Krishna and Arjun on the field of battle.

Now, people often get confused: if Krishna and Arjun had such a long conversation on the battlefield itself, how come nobody else could see what they were discussing? How come they could talk so much, how come they could search into the highest spiritual truths and yet not be noticed upon the battlefield?

The truth of the matter is that, from the mystical perspective, the whole episode of the Gita is a spiritual vision within which Krishna and Arjun communicate. They communicate at the level of the mystical, the astral, *the timeless moment that is beyond human time.* In an instant of what we would consider to be a moment of human time, comes about the complete transformation of Arjun. Human or terrestrial moments are not the only measure of time: we know through science (most particularly through Albert Einstein's theories) that time is relative.

The idea of the Gita is that if you really wish it, if you're really able to gather all your energies into calling the Divine to help you, your entire vision can be expanded in just the blink of an eye! Just as Arjun's vision expanded on the battlefield of Kurukshetra.

25. The greatest power in the world is the power of meditative action. This is Krishna's entire secret of Karma Yoga or the yoga of action. He is enabling Arjun to act in a state of being that is meditative. He enables Arjun to fight the war and shoot his arrows in a meditative state. This is the highest state of the warrior. In fact, this state of the warrior is described in different traditions of the world, such as in the Buddhist martial traditions, exemplified by the Bushido code of Japan's ancient samurai. This idea of inward calmness, meditativeness even in the midst of the most dynamic decisive action, is of the nature of the Divine. It is eventually the quality of consciousness that you are acting with, that determines the spiritual fruit you gain from it. And Krishna is a master at this: enabling Arjun to make his actions move from the mundane to the sacred, from the violent to the divine, from the ordinary to the extraordinary.

26. Never get caught up in the morass of negativities about life. Life is a constant flow.

Sometimes, the water in the river has to flow over rocks. And sometimes, it hurtles down a cliff, as a waterfall. The flow of life has a rhythm in itself. It moves through stages.

Hence, never get caught up in what you believe to be negative: that is simply another moment for exploring the path. In the spirit of the Upanishads, *"Charaiveti Charaiveti"*: no matter what, keep walking on, keep moving on. This idea is also echoed by Gautam Buddha. This very attitude is the most rewarding when it comes to difficult situations in life.

27. Surrender yourself to the universal energy. This is the yoga of *saranagati*. It is the very spirit of the Gita. Eventually, Arjun has to surrender his whole being, his whole action, all of himself, to the Greater! Sometimes life deals us such a situation that we have no option but to surrender. Surrendering then, to the Divine, is the only way! This has been the way of the highest mystics, not only in India, but throughout the world. Life is bigger than us. The Divine is infinitely larger than us. We must be like children—

surrendering to the moment, abandoning our sense of anxiety, worry, and letting existence take its own course. This is the spiritual way which Arjun is encouraged to adopt by Krishna. And so doing, his ego or ahamkara is dropped. And when you drop the ego, you're able to deal with all situations in the way they most correctly need to be dealt with.

28. Ultimately, the text of the Gita is all about awakening. To awaken to the true gigantic power within ourselves is the very essence of the entire spiritual message which Krishna is giving Arjun. Never think otherwise: even if the whole world is telling you that things are bad, that things are not solvable! Believe in the immensity of the Divine's grace which dwells within you. That will give you the utmost courage to overcome all odds in life! It's all about self-faith, which leads to deeper faith (*vishvaasa/shraddha*) in life itself.

29. Krishna tells Arjun very clearly that what we think to be life is but *an illusory dream* (the play of Maya). Our perception is usually quite limited: *ultimate reality is not entirely in consonance*

with what we believe, with what our conditioning tells us about life. Ultimate reality is about *waking from the dreams of mind* and realizing the great vastness of spiritual truth that is existent within all things. This is a question of not being "taught" as much as being able to transcend our psychological limitations on the way we look at life. *Remove psychological limitations from yourself!* The whole of the Bhagvad Gita is actually about the removal of psychological limitations of Arjun, because when those are removed, only then are you able to look at life with an eye of greater bliss, greater realization, greater consciousness, and a greater ability to act for one's own good as well as for the greater good. And that, ultimately, determines how well you are able to deal with the tough times in life.

Great People on the Bhagvad Gita

Great people throughout history have had very enlightening things to say about the Mahabharat and the Bhagvad Gita. For example, Swami

Vivekananda says that the Bhagvad Gita is a bouquet composed of the beautiful flowers of the spiritual truths collected from the Upanishads. The great philosopher Wilhelm von Humboldt has said: "The Gita is perhaps the only truly philosophical song existing in any known language, perhaps the deepest and loftiest thing the world has known."

The yogi Paramahansa Yogananda says that the Bhagvad Gita's essence is right action, non-attachment, and unity with god. Swami Chinmayananda has described the Bhagvad Gita as the very essence of Vedanta. The German mystic Rudolf Steiner has said: "In order to approach a creation as sublime as the Bhagvad Gita with full understanding, it is necessary to attune our soul to it."

The lessons of the Gita have great appeal to people across the ages because of certain profound ideas: the idea of finding spiritual purity, greater purpose, and higher consciousness, of cultivating meditativeness, and of manifesting our highest energies in thought and action.

The profound scientist and intellectual J Robert Oppenheimer said: "The juxtaposition of Western civilization's most terrifying scientific achievement with the most dazzling description of the mystical experience has been given to us by the Bhagvad Gita, India's greatest literary monument. The Bhagvad Gita is the most beautiful philosophical song existing in any known tongue." Oppenheimer was key in the invention of the atom bomb, and paid a huge tribute to the Bhagvad Gita by saying the following upon witnessing the first test of the atom bomb: "We knew the world would not be the same. Few people laughed, few people cried, most people were silent. I remembered the line from the Hindu scripture, the Bhagvad Gita. Vishnu is trying to persuade the Prince that he should do his duty and to impress him takes on his multi-armed form and says, 'Now I am become Death, the destroyer of worlds.' I suppose we all thought that, one way or another." (Also, rather cryptically, Oppenheimer once said that the atom bomb of the twentieth century was *the first one in the modern age*: he might have been referring to a previous atomic age and nuclear weaponry as hinted at within the Mahabharat).

The Gita generates self-wisdom and self-silence, and that is its beauty. The great Hermann Hesse, the author of *Siddhartha*, has said: "The marvel of the Bhagvad Gita is its truly beautiful revelation of life's wisdom which enables philosophy to blossom into religion."

Charles Elliott has called the Mahabharat a greater poem than *The Iliad*, and the famous philosopher Will Durant has emphatically affirmed the same idea.

Bal Gangadhar Tilak was fond of saying that the Gita was not about people who renounced life, but for those who were living material lives yet looking towards enlightenment! Dada Vaswani says that the Gita is all about courage, heroism, and the strength of the soul, or *Atma Shakti*.

The great western philosopher Henry David Thoreau was ecstatic upon receiving the Gita. He describes it as a unique experience, saying: "In the morning I bathe my intellect in the stupendous and cosmogonal philosophy of the Bhagvad Gita, since whose composition years of the gods have elapsed, and in comparison with which our modern world and its literature seem puny and trivial. I doubt if that philosophy is not to be referred to a previous state of existence, so remote is its sublimity from our conceptions. I lay down the book and go to my well for water, and there I meet the servant of the Brahmin, priest of Brahma and Vishnu and Indra, who still sits in his temple on the Ganges reading the Vedas, or dwells at the root of a tree with his crust and water jug. I meet his servant come to draw water for his master, and our buckets as it were grate together in the same well. The pure water is mingled with the sacred water of the Ganges."

The Gita's enlightening aspects, Krishna's playful yet profound spiritual stance, the idea that *perfection already dwells within the atma or soul:* these concepts have had tremendous appeal to people throughout the world, over millennia!

George Russell has said that the Gita and the Upanishads contain great fullness of wisdom. Sarvepalli Radhakrishnan, the erstwhile president of India, has called it more than just religious or philosophical, more than an esoteric spiritual text. The great Swami Rama has said the Bhagvad Gita is the very fountainhead of Eastern psychology.

Indeed, the Gita is not just about spirituality. It is a text on deep psychology as well.

Helena Roerich has said: "I am so fond of a statement in the Bhagvad Gita, this finest pearl of the Eastern writings, that I never tire of repeating it, and so I shall quote it to you as well: 'Man comes to Me by various paths, but by whatever path man comes to Me, on that path I welcome him, for all paths are Mine.'"

The totality of the Gita's teachings, and its bridging of the mystical and material aspects of life, is unmatched in its appeal to great people.

Nehru said, "The Bhagvad Gita is the spiritual foundation of existence itself. It keeps in view the point of action, yet regards our spiritual nature and grander purpose within the cosmos."

We must remember that it's the Gita's message of hope, of love, and trust, that has had universal resonance. It is poetic yet liberates us from all the conditioned knowledge that we are subject to on an everyday basis and which we accumulate like dust upon the mind. The Gita washes this dust clean, like the river Ganga is said to purify us at all three levels of being: mind, body and soul!

The very respected nationalist Madan Mohan Malaviya has said that the Bhagvad Gita is the book of the truest knowledge, calling upon self-control, non-violence, truth, compassion, obedience to duty, and fighting against adharma or unrighteousness. He has said that there is no book in the entire range of the world's literature as high as the Bhagvad Gita. That it is not just for Hindus but for the entire mankind.

The mystic CW Leadbeater has talked about *bhakti* or the divine attitude of devotion, through reading the Gita. He has described it as filling him with a thrill of ecstasy, and also enlightening him in terms of evolution, both intellectual and spiritual. Again, Leadbeater has talked about the Bhagvad Gita as being all about the doctrine of love. Leadbeater says: "The disciple Arjun, to whom the Guru spoke, was a great lover of mankind; according to the scripture this great soldier sank down upon the floor of his chariot before the battle of Kurukshetra began, full of sorrow because he loved his enemies and could not bear to injure them. The teacher Krishna then explained to him, amid much philosophical teaching, that the greatest thing in life is service, that God Himself is the greatest server—for He keeps the wheel of life revolving, not because any benefit can possibly accrue to Him in consequence, but for the sake of the world—and that men should follow His example and work for the welfare of mankind. Many great ones, He said, had reached perfection by following this path of life, by doing their duty without personal desire. To love without ceasing is the way of the second ray; in the Gita it is shown how this love should be directed to men and other beings in Karma Yoga (the yoga by action or work) and to God in Bhakti Yoga (the yoga by devotion)."

The Gita talks of spirituality as *an inner science,* and not outward rituals. As such, even the greatest logicians and intellectuals can relate to it. The great philosophical author Aldous Huxley has described the Gita in this manner: "It is the most systematic statement of spiritual evolution of endowing value to mankind. It is one of the most clear and comprehensive summaries of perennial philosophy ever revealed; hence its enduring value is subject not only to India but to all of humanity."

Even people who are otherwise well-known for material pursuits and power play, have been deeply moved by the Gita's effect of inner silence and sublimity. For example, Warren Hastings has said, quite surprisingly, "I don't hesitate to pronounce the Gita a performance of great originality, of sublimity of conception, reasoning and diction almost unequalled; and a single exception, amongst all the known religions of mankind."

The Gita effortlessly bridges psychology and spirituality, literary poetry and mystical poetry! Mahatma Gandhi has said: "When doubts haunt me, when disappointments stare me in the face, and

I see not one ray of hope on the horizon, I turn to the Bhagvad Gita and find a verse to comfort me; and I immediately begin to smile in the midst of overwhelming sorrow."

The power of the Gita is in making us aware of the unchanging witness of all things: the soul as the foundation of our existence, which calmly observes the workings of the world. Most eloquently does Sri Aurobindo, the profound sage or rishi of modern India, say: "The Bhagvad Gita is a true scripture of the human race, a living creation rather than a book, with a new message for every age and a new meaning for every civilization."

He goes on to say: "The thought of the Gita is not pure monism although it sees in one unchanging, pure, eternal Self the foundation of all cosmic existence, nor Mayavada, although it speaks of the Maya of the three modes of Prakriti omnipresent in the created world; nor is it qualified Monism although it places in the One his eternal supreme Prakriti manifested in the form of the *Jiva* and lays most stress on dwelling in God rather than dissolution as the supreme state of spiritual consciousness; nor is it Sankhya although it explains the created world by the double principle of Purusha and Prakriti; nor is it Vaishnava theism although it presents to us Krishna, who is the Avatara of Vishnu according to the Puranas, as the supreme Deity and allows no essential difference nor any actual superiority of the status of the indefinable relationless Brahman over that of this Lord of beings who is the Master of the universe and the Friend of all creatures. Like the earlier spiritual synthesis of the Upanishads, this later synthesis, at once spiritual and intellectual, avoids naturally every such rigid determination as would injure its universal comprehensiveness. Its aim is precisely the opposite to that of the polemist commentators who found this Scripture established as one of the three highest Vedantic authorities and attempted to turn it into a weapon of offence and defence against other schools and systems. The Gita is not a weapon for dialectical warfare; it is a gate opening on the whole world of spiritual truth and experience and the view it gives us embraces all the provinces of that supreme region. It maps out, but it does not cut up or build walls or hedges to confine our vision."

The celebrated personality Annie Besant has said: "Among the priceless teachings that may be found in the great Indian epic Mahabharat, there is none so rare and priceless as the Gita. This is the India of which I speak—the India which, as I said, is to me the Holy Land. For those who, though born for this life in a Western land, and clad in a Western body, can yet look back to earlier incarnations in which they drank the milk of spiritual wisdom from the breast of their true mother—they must feel ever the magic of her immemorial past; must dwell ever under the spell of her deathless fascination; for they are bound to India by all the sacred memories of their past and with her, too, are bound up all the radiant hopes of their future, a future which they know they will share with her who is their true mother in the soul-life." Further, she has said, summing up the Gita's message: "That the spiritual man need not be a recluse, that union with the divine life may be achieved and maintained in the midst of worldly affairs, that the obstacles to that union lie not outside us but within us—such is the central lesson of the Bhagvad Gita."

To quote the great philosopher Ralph Waldo Emerson: "I owed a magnificent day to the Bhagvad Gita. It was as if an empire spoke to us, nothing small or unworthy, but large, serene, consistent, the voice of an old intelligence which in another age and climate had pondered and thus disposed of the same questions which exercise us."

The Uniqueness of the Mahabharat and the Bhagvad Gita

We can see how these scriptures are unique! After all, where would you have a text which, on the battlefield, would expound the greatest truth, as in the episode of the Bhagvad Gita within the Mahabharat? Where would you have an episode that happened between Bheeshma and Yudhishthir, wherein Bheeshma prolongs his dying moments so that he can distil the essence of Sankhya philosophy in the Upanishads to educate Yudhishthir on what it means to be a great leader, a great king.

In other words, the Mahabharat encompasses the greatest contradictions of life—the material and the spiritual—and puts them into a particular oneness, no more so than in the Bhagvad Gita. It is always fruitful to look at the main teachings, the very diamonds, that the Bhagvad Gita enlightens us with!

CHAPTER-4

Main Characters and Events

In all great human stories, there are a few characters who are outstanding. They are on their own spiritual quest and material journeys, yet personify our own quest also. Ultimately, to know ourselves more deeply—at both the spiritual and material levels—is the ultimate aim of this quest.

In the Mahabharat, as in life in general, there are no black and whites: nobody is ultimately inferior or superior (for example, even the so-called villain Duryodhan exhibits some rare virtues, and the Pandav heroes have to repent and bear hell too. The great guru of the martial arts, Dronacharya, is often culpable of partiality, while a primarily negative character like Shakuni displays valour in battle!).

We can see that within the Mahabharat are key characters we can identify with: people who go through the trials and tribulations of *all* human beings, and through their paths show us how we ourselves are to deal with tough times in life.

The Mahabharat is filled with characters who teach us much about how to transcend life's various difficulties: the difficulties could be related to relationships, work, position in life, success, and so on.

Eventually, the Mahabharat is a story about conflict—conflict deep within man's own heart, and conflict with others! There are a few personalities who are very poignant, and whose stories are very moving. Such a story in the Mahabharat is the story of Kunti—the mother of the Pandavs—and her eldest son Karna whom she had to part with in his very infancy.

Kunti and Karna

Kunti and Karna represent both the poignancy and power of the Mahabharat. They are two characters who are at a crossroads: Karna is Kunti's eldest son, yet is fighting against her other Pandav sons! This very idea places Kunti and Karna at the centrepiece of the Mahabharat's dramatic action, and through their relationship we can begin to understand the profound implications of the epic in entirety, in a condensed and unique way: reconciling the material and spiritual dilemmas that all the characters face in this epic.

You see, Kunti had abandoned her firstborn Karna. And that has been a very emotional chapter in all of Indian tradition, because Karna grew up without knowing who his real parents were. Had he been accepted by Kunti, he would have been the eldest of the Pandav brothers—he would have been the inheritor of the crown also. But in his own difficult way, Karna grew up. He became a great warrior. He became a great fighter. In fact, it is very touching that before the battle of Kurukshetra, Kunti and Karna meet and they speak about many things. Kunti tells Karna that actually he was born a prince, that she gave birth to him; and Karna asserts that his real parents are the charioteer Adhiratha and his wife Radha—people who brought him up after Kunti had cruelly abandoned him.

Now, Kunti is very worried that Karna will kill her sons in battle—the five Pandav brothers who are *publicly known* to be her sons. And she's questioning Karna about why he does not *join* the Pandavs, his *real* brothers, and why he is insistent upon taking the side of the evil Duryodhan, their Kaurav cousin who is fighting the Pandavs.

Yet Karna is very clear: he treats Duryodhan as his own brother. He treats him as a true friend. Duryodhan has shown him kindness, so he will stand by Duryodhan in this difficult situation. So, this is the first lesson we learn from Karna. He is very steadfast in his devotion to people who have stood by him during tough times! This is something we must remember: never abandon those who stood by you when others gave up on you! This is why Karna is regarded as a very noble persona in all of Indian tradition. He does not just go to the side of gain or profit. He is very clearly on the side that *has not abandoned him, that has believed in him.* And those are the people who are truly precious. Even if by worldly standards they are not considered very "good", but their belief in you makes them a valuable part of your journey upon earth. Never abandon them!

The second thing to understand is that Karna is not craving the crown. You see, Kunti tells him that the Pandavs will win the war and then they'll get the crown, they'll get the kingdom, and Karna will become the king simply because he's the eldest of the brothers. But Karna does not fall for that. He says that he cannot discard his sense of loyalty to Duryodhan and the Kauravs because they have given him a home in their hearts! And he's very clear that if he goes to the Pandavs and Arjun's side, it will look like cowardice, it will look like he's getting away from facing the might of the great warriors Arjun and Bheem. Karna is ready to die but he'll not break his promise. That is the way *we* must be. We must have *integrity*!

The Kauravs are depending on Karna to stand up to the mighty Arjun on the other side. And because of that reason, he is very clear about what he must do on the field of battle. Kunti requests him to spare the lives of all the Pandavs, knowing how strong a warrior he is. Karna gives her his word that he will not harm the four Pandavs: Yudhishthir, Bheem, Nakula, or Sahadeva. But he cannot give his word for Arjun! Apart from Arjun, he promises to do as Kunti requests. And Karna's promise is taken to be writ in gold: it is a solid promise, twenty-four carat gold!

Karna's promise is known throughout Indian tradition to have the strength and integrity that is greater than anybody else's. That is why Karna is revered as a hero. For all his personal faults, he is still regarded very highly in Indian spirituality because when he gives his word, you can be sure to rely on it!

This is another learning we must absorb from the character of Karna. His word, his promise has integrity, and that is the way we must be. Don't be fickle! If you can't keep your promise, if you can't keep your word, you are not worth anything. That is the first step towards truth. And from truth comes consciousness. From consciousness comes bliss or ananda. So, in the mystic formula of India, Sat-Chit-Ananda, *Sat or truth* is the first word. And Karna is a paragon of that.

Kunti, the mother of the Pandavs, is herself a product of so many difficulties in her life. She signifies the greatest energies of spiritual attainment as well as dealing with tough material circumstances. She has gone through all sorts of arduous situations in life.

There have been some women throughout history who have been the real movers behind events. So, too, in this epic of India. Kunti, while seeming to a lot of people to be not so pivotal, is actually at the very crux of the Mahabharat. She is a veritable "all-rounder", proficient and very well regarded by the general population, respected by sages and kings, looked upon as the ideal mother to her five great sons! But at the same time, Kunti has many levels. She has been through so much in her life!

She was once said to express this thought:

"It is better to be a burning flame and quickly finish with the business of life
Than to exist as a damp, weak flicker that creates more smoke than fire."

Through this very thought of Kunti, we can gauge her prowess. She believes in taking quick decisions. The purport of what she is saying is this: *she believes in making the lamp of life burn with great intensity!*

This is the advice she gives to her son Yudhishthir, who is in two minds of whether to fight the war of Kurukshetra or to become a renunciate, an ascetic. Similarly, she advises Krishna also (who happens to be her nephew), when Krishna comes to mediate peace at the court of Hastinapur. The lesson we learn from her is that it is very important to act decisively and clearly. This decisiveness and clarity of mind signifies the essence of what Kunti is. And it is a great lesson for us when we are facing our own crucial moments.

The question of whether *to wage the war of the Mahabharat or not* is the pivotal question. Kunti says if that is the only honourable recourse left, that if there is a choice between dishonour and combat, then a fight is necessary, war is necessary. Yes, Kunti has been treated dishonourably for many years. She has borne that shame nobly, but she is also a very fearless person! Kunti signifies the kind of person who is not afraid to do the noble thing—to create peace, to have affection for all, and so on. But when it comes to justice, like a true Kshatriya woman she gathers courage, and she drops fear. That is the whole meaning of Dharma.

Dharma

The concept of Dharma is crucial to the Mahabharat. It will be useful to understand the essence of Dharma through the character of Kunti.

The concept of Dharma and royal duty is perhaps best personified by Kunti. She does feel agitated by the prospect of war: with the possibility of her sons dying, the sons she has brought up with so much love and care, without a father to take care of them.

And especially finding Karna, Duryodhan, and the others intent upon destroying her sons and their whole lineage, makes Kunti nervous but does not shake her decision about going ahead with war. She is afraid to lose her sons, but she always maintains that honour is more important. We *must remember this* while we deal with our own challenges. We must never shirk from doing the honourable thing. Even Gautama Buddha used to talk about this quality of being noble within: noble courage, the feeling of *arya*. The word arya is very important in the Indian lexicon: be it in Hinduism/Sanatan Dharma, Buddhism, or other spiritual paths. It means acting with nobility, decisiveness, dynamism: walking the path even if you must walk it alone! It is like the great poet of India, Rabindranath Tagore has said: "*Ekla Cholo Re*"—Walk on alone. Even if you have nobody to walk with you, walk fearlessly alone! This echoes the old dictum of the Upanishads and Vedanta philosophy: Charaiveti Charaiveti—keep moving on, keep walking forward, with dynamism!

Again, what we have learnt from Kunti is that she's willing to make supreme sacrifices even at the risk of making her eldest son Karna further estranged. When it came to saving the clan (because the alternative was banishment, embarrassment for the entire clan, because Karna was born outside wedlock before she was married to Pandu), she renounced her most loved firstborn.

Sometimes, even that *toughness is needed in life.* While it may seem cruel, the larger picture is important. We must each, in our individual capacity, *be prepared to make sacrifices,* even if it pains our hearts. Through these two characters—Karna and Kunti—we can see all the factors about facing times in life that are tough, but overcoming them through the power of inward determination, and inward courage. These qualities are the very essence of *dharma*!

We can see dharmic essence running through Kunti's life. She had a very tough life. From her youth, she was pampered as the favourite of her father, King Surasena. She was called Pritha. She was entrusted with very key tasks. Her father's friend, King Kuntibhoja (the king of the Kunti kingdom), pleaded with her father to be allowed to adopt her, as he had no children of his own. So she was given away: at such a tender age, she had to move away from her kith and kin, her childhood friends and siblings. She was taken to a foreign land, in the land of King Kuntibhoja—who really loved her as his own daughter.

Such a young girl had to face the anguish of separation from her loved ones—this shaped Kunti's character for years to come. Like they say, *it is the test of time and circumstance that makes us who we are!*

It is said of Kunti:

"My life has not the joy of a river's water,
Which flows with one stream of energy,
Moving as it likes, free and unrestricted . . .
But is like the water in a lake
I must take the shape of the domain I am placed in
Expected to adapt, to fit in, to fulfil the demands
of all."

Kunti was regarded even by Krishna as having the ability to adapt to all situations. And the ability to adapt to all situations is indeed the very key to adapting to tough situations in life.

That is why Kunti is regarded as an exemplar of the highest virtues when it comes to excellence in the face of adversity.

At a young age, Kunti made a place for herself in King Kuntibhoja's household and royal court. She was given immense respect. She earned it. She was exceptional, intelligent, pure, generous. She ran the royal household. She received and honoured guests. But she was also cursed with a terrible destiny. You see, it once happened that the fiery sage Durvasa visited the household of Kuntibhoja. Now, Durvasa was somebody everybody feared, because he took offence at one's slightest mistake and was known to even curse the people who offended him.

So, King Kuntibhoja didn't know what to do. How could he keep this sage from losing his temper? How could he accord him such hospitality that would keep him in good spirits, that would make him bless the household instead of cursing it? Then he saw his daughter and he realized that she is the best and wisest person to take charge of the situation. And indeed, Kunti made sure that the sage's accommodation was perfect, that he had no discomfort, that he didn't get angry. By the end of his visit, the sage was so pleased that he gave Kunti a blessing and a boon!

The boon was that she could summon the deities at will, and could choose to have children by them. This is a very great power but Durvasa gave it to a young girl. This led to its own consequences. One day, Kunti looked at the Sun (Suryadev or the Sun God) and got transfixed. She enunciated the incantation that was told to her by Durvasa. Suryadev appeared, and thereby Kunti was impregnated with the seed of Karna within her. Her whole childhood was in a way shattered. She had to now choose whether to live in the shame of being an unwed mother, or give up her only child!

Eventually, Kunti made the difficult decision of protecting the reputation of her royal household. Karna would have been called an illegitimate child. And Kunti was conscious about the infamy this would bring upon the household of King Kuntibhoja. So, she put Karna on a basket and set him afloat on a river. He was then discovered and adopted by the charioteer Adhiratha.

Hence, from a mythological sense, Karna's material fate was sealed from the start. He was of the highest birth possible: his father was the divine Suryadev, the Sun God, his mother was the great Kunti. Yet, all his life, he was cursed by being called one of low birth. He was left, even as an infant, to the mercy of the elements. So his shame, his anger (krodha), is understandable. It gives us much insight into his actions within the Mahabharat. There are times he does feel sorry for himself. There are times when he feels psychologically down and out! And we absolutely cannot expect a person who has gone through so much hardship as a child, to act nobly all the time.

The symbol or metaphor of the Sun God played a very important part in Karna's life: it runs through the Mahabharat. He worshipped the Sun from a young age. He is said to have the radiance of the Sun on his persona. Having a splendid, golden-hued personality is the way Karna is described. His was originally a very dharmic path.

The Contest of Arms (*Astra Pariksha*) and Other Factors

Kunti was promised by Suryadev that Karna would be taken care of. She missed the growing years of Karna and feels guilty that she could not be there to nurture him as a mother should, to teach him, to give him love. All through his life, Karna has been made to go through challenges. The episode of the contest of arms or Astra Pariksha within the Mahabharat is very important. It was to test the prowess, the martial skills of the royal households. The Kauravs took part. The Pandavs took part. And even Karna took part.

Eventually, Karna's turn came to face up to Arjun, the great warrior from the Pandav side. And it was when they were about to clash that Kunti had an episode of fainting. She could not bear the thought that two of her sons would harm each other!

Karna had to go through numerous insults in his life. In particular, Bheem used to call him a person of low caste. And Bheem encouraged Arjun to refuse Karna's challenge! So Karna was insulted and shamed at every opportunity. It is only Duryodhan who crowned him the king of Anga so that he would have the status to fight the Kshatriya Prince Arjun. Duryodhan extended a hand of friendship. Eventually, during the clash with Arjun in the context of archery, they both matched each other, arrow for arrow. And it seemed like Karna would win; but eventually the contest was stopped.

Kunti feels that Duryodhan is using Karna for his own adharmic and selfish ends; because he knows that only the might of Karna's martial prowess would be able to defeat the Pandavs. Karna however does not harbour doubts about his friendship with Duryodhan. He believes in being dharmic, in being a noble ally. He believes in being a true brother in spirit, he believes in reciprocating the honour that he has received from Duryodhan. Yet, there are often times he feels like a victim. For example, the great Guru Dronacharya, who is the martial teacher of all the princes and of Karna, is actually guilty of mistreating Karna.

Dronacharya, War, and Weaponry

There were certain esoteric weapons, such as the *Brahmastra*, which are described in the Mahabharat. Now, Dronacharya gave the knowledge of those to Arjun, but he chose not to give them to Karna! Perhaps Guru Dronacharya had his own reasons: he found Arjun trustworthy, having the right mindset to handle such dangerous weapons. He regarded Arjun as having that coolness of being, that wisdom of intelligence, that nobility of character that would put the weapons to good use and not misuse them, as Karna may have! Because Karna was more volatile in temper: he was more easily aggravated, etc.

Weaponry in the Mahabharat is very interesting because it describes how there are certain weapons which can cause large-scale destruction. In a way, the Mahabharat echoes the nuclear age. There are descriptions of mushroom-shaped explosions also! Well, that is another discussion. The idea of warrior-hood in the Kshatriya tradition is one of inward purity and nobility of purpose. And in that sense Arjun is the perfect warrior, because he does not get perturbed by personal motivations as such. He believes in fighting on the side of right. That is Arjun's character. And Arjun himself is a most interesting character in the Mahabharat.

Arjun

Arjun is regarded as a peerless archer and warrior. But at the same time, throughout his life, he has gone through numerous difficulties, not only in his exile with his Pandav brothers but even later on in his many travels and exiles (incognito) throughout the land. He was in fact a person of great asceticism, of renunciation. There were many years in his life which he spent in meditative trance, in the seeking of higher truth. And these are part of the reasons why Krishna chose Arjun for expounding the Bhagvad Gita. In fact, not only the Bhagvad Gita, there are two other instances within the Mahabharat when Krishna has chosen to speak to Arjun about the highest spiritual truth. There is not just the Bhagvad Gita, but also the Anu Gita, and then the Uttara Gita.

Arjun's character is one which signifies pure courage. He's in harmony and on the path of Dharma. That is the ideal of true warrior-hood in the ancient teachings of Sanatan Dharma of India.

Arjun signifies the kind of leadership which has come out of non-egoic nobility of heart and mind, clarity of heart and mind. It is an enduring lesson for today! Such a one as Arjun can be trusted with the greatest power of weapons. This is in contrast to the self-seeking egomaniacs throughout the world who are sitting pretty on nuclear buttons. The most terrible nuclear power has been entrusted to the wrong people. And that has been used for destructive ends in humanity's history. Arjun is one who does not believe in being a prince who revels in luxury. He's as comfortable in a palace as he is in a hut as a chaste hermit.

These are lessons Arjun has deeply absorbed from his mother Kunti. You see, Kunti is a great queen of the Kuru dynasty. But when she married Prince Pandu, she was not even welcomed properly into the capital city of Hastinapur. She did not get her due as a *Raj Mata* or queen. Even the great Bheeshma, who's said to be the protector of the throne and who had great personal regard for Kunti, urged Pandu to marry Maadri. A capable person like Kunti is always a threat to the ambitions of others! And that is a patriarchal understanding which has permeated throughout world history.

The Pandavs

Once Pandu married Maadri, his affections towards her increased. And he found himself spending more time with Maadri than with Kunti. There was playfulness, affection in their relationship. Kunti, on the other hand, had to endure a rather lonely life.

Now, Pandu is an interesting character because he handed over the kingdom to his blind brother Dhritarashtra, even though he was the heir apparent. Pandu went into the forest with his wives. He led a life of renunciation, s*anyaas*, or asceticism. Deep within nature, they nurtured their children, the Pandavs. Eventually, Kunti invoked the incantations when she realized that children were not forthcoming. She had three sons: Yudhishthir the wise and the eldest, whose father was Lord Dharmaraja who is regarded traditionally as the dispenser of divine justice and the epitome of *sadaachaara* or right conduct; Bheem the strong, the second Pandav, whose father was said to be Vayu the lord of air; and the third son Arjun, the matchless warrior whose father was Indra, the king of the demigods.

Pandu entreated upon Kunti to tell her the sacred incantation, because he himself was incapable of fatherhood. Maadri used the mantra and to her was born the handsome Nakula and the most brilliant Sahadeva. And the greatness of Kunti is that she always treated these two as her very own, making no distinction between Yudhishthir, Bheem, Arjun, Nakul, and Sahadeva. Now, we can understand that Karna would be extremely aggrieved of this situation, because perhaps Pandu would have accepted him in his household. But Kunti chose to hide the fact that Karna was her son. However, she knew that Karna was living a good life with Radha and Adhiratha who—even though poor—had nobility of heart.

The five Pandav brothers themselves faced much deprivation and injustice, being sent to the forests for their long exile through the evil machinations of Duryodhan and the Kauravs. Yet, they never really complained, they were never bitter. Everything was snatched from their deserving hands. And Karna also played his part in siding with the Kauravs. Karna is a fearless warrior, a peerless archer, a great friend of Duryodhan, and becomes the Raja of Anga, but at times he too can feel bitter about life.

The sole goal of Duryodhan became to destroy the Pandavs and their mother, by sending them away from the capital city of Hastinapur to Varnavat. The whole shameful episode of setting the mansion of lacquer (*laakshagriha*) on fire while Kunti and her sons were within it, stands apart as a most despicable episode!

Dhritarashtra

These kinds of conspiracies, as described above, are a constant refrain in the Pandavs' life. And unfortunately, their uncle King Dhritarashtra, who's supposed to be protecting them, was poisoned by the wily and twisted counsel of his evil-minded minister Kanik—who taught him the ways of deception, assassination, and deceit!

King Dhritarashtra, in fact, signifies a king who is blinded by his love for his selfish kith and kin, such as Duryodhan. He falls into a conspiracy with his son Duryodhan and wants to destroy the unsuspecting wife and children of his honourable brother Pandu. It is, however, a very interesting character within the Mahabharat, Vidura—the half-brother of Pandu and Dhritarashtra—who saves the day by giving the Pandavs and Kunti the information that the conspiracy was afoot to burn them within their mansion in the forest.

Alerted by Vidura, the Pandavs escaped the fire, when everybody thought that they had perished within it. They disguised themselves and wandered the land, waiting for the opportune moment for their return. Hence, Karna, in a way, escapes the terrible fate of becoming a murderer! It is this seething anger within Karna, engendered by being treated as an inferior by the sons of Kunti and by the masters and mentors, which ignited the hate within his heart. Yet, he is not the only one who has flaws within the Mahabharat. Kunti herself resorts to cleverness when she substitutes a poor Nishaad woman and her five sons in place of the six of them, so that people would think that they are dead. She sends six innocents to their death! A highly questionable act, though done to protect her family.

Draupadi

The great beauty of the Mahabharat is that it says nobody is perfect! Everybody has foibles. Everybody has faults. In that way, the Mahabharat is a very mature work of tradition. For example, the great wife of the Pandav brothers, Draupadi, signifies this duality of character within all. She insulted Karna at her wedding ceremony—did not let him contest for her during the *Swayamvara* ceremony, during which Karna could have won the day and taken her to be his bride. (Karna always felt mocked by the pride of Draupadi. And in a way, this became pivotal in the whole narrative of the ill relations between the Kauravs and the Pandavs).

Now, Draupadi's character is one of the most interesting in all of tradition. She is said to be tremendously beautiful, alluring, a dark-skinned beauty who created passions in men's hearts and desire deep within their souls. She was coveted as a bride. And the greatest warriors of the land had gathered in her father King Drupad's court, in the land of Panchal, to win her hand. And keep in mind that Draupadi was not only just a paragon of the feminine form: she was said to be so intensely intelligent that she could put even the most learned scholars to shame.

During the contest of arms, within which warriors would compete for the princess' hand, there was an unfair condition. It implied that only one of noble birth, or so-called high birth, was eligible to be proclaimed a victor. This excluded Karna, naturally, as he was regarded a sut-putra or a lowly charioteer's son.

But another interesting thing happened. The five Pandav brothers, who were assumed to have died in the fire at Varnavrat, came to Panchal in disguise, pretending to be Brahmins. They disguised themselves so that Arjun, the matchless warrior, could win and take Draupadi to be his bride.

Draupadi was so enchanting! She was the one who actually unified the joint energy of the Pandav brothers. She kept them together. Else, it very often happens that brothers fall apart. But the one blot on Draupadi is that she rebuked Karna by saying "*Naham varayami sutam*," implying she will not marry a mere charioteer's son and not allowing him to take part in the contest of archery. With that, Karna's hopes and dreams were shattered.

At the swayamvar of Draupadi, it was eventually Arjun who strung the bow, shot the mark, and won the day. He got married to Draupadi. Thereafter, she became the wife of all five brothers: she became the muse of fortune to the entire Pandav household. She loved Arjun. Even though she was carelessly chosen to be the wife of all five by Kunti due to an inadvertent slip of tongue, she played her part dutifully, faithfully, uncomplainingly.

It is a testament to Draupadi's strength that she speaks up so boldly for herself, post the shameful episode of the *vastra-haran* (disrobing). She displays the highest valour and moral courage even when everyone seems to have lost that. Draupadi personifies the highest virtues of womanhood and human character: guts, speaking out against injustice, integrity, and the effort of instilling moral consciousness within those who need to exercise it.

The Crisis Situation

The contest of gambling between the Pandav and Kaurav brothers stands apart as one of the most definitive turning points of the Mahabharat. It is the pivotal moment that precipitates the crisis at the heart of this epic.

It is especially difficult to understand Yudhishthir's motivations in putting to stake all his brothers, and more than anything else their wife

Draupadi, who they eventually stand to lose at that game of dice which Duryodhan has very cunningly crafted along with his maternal uncle Shakuni!

What is most disgraceful about the whole episode is the way Draupadi is attempted to be stripped of her every inch of clothing. She could have been made to stand denuded by the Kauravs (vastra haran/*cheer haran*) but for the timely intervention of Krishna! Krishna rescues her from that distress, through the mystic power of his divine yoga.

Yet the whole idea is that the land of Bharat (from which the word "Mahabharat" takes its name), was never the same after that incident, because whilst brothers could fight and warriors could fight at war, a woman being so disgraced in front of everybody completely changed the circumstances! On that day itself, the unfortunate destiny of the Kauravs was written. It was stamped and concluded. It was known that it would end in their slaughter! Bad fortune always follows those who don't know how to honour women. This is a very important societal and political learning from the Mahabharat.

Honour

We must understand that women should never be dishonoured in any way. Draupadi was deprived of her honour at the court of King Dhritarashtra, where all the nobles stood mute, including the brave Bheeshma. This very act is brutal! The ancient texts of India say very clearly that wherever women are dishonoured, from that land the Divine withdraws His grace, His blessing. Whenever women are shamed, that age becomes a dark one. There are several verses in the Mahabharat that endorse this.

Yet, even in today's world, people strip women of honour, rob them of grace. Then how can we expect well-being and prosperity for all? In fact, the tough times and most distressing times of the Mahabharat take place after this disgraceful conduct towards Draupadi.

So we must understand the lesson that as long as women are treated as mere offerings on the altar of manhood, we are in for great trouble as a society. After this incident, the Pandavs swore revenge. And then, they were banished into the forest for thirteen long years. Luckily, Draupadi was saved from that whole situation of complete dishonour, by Krishna's grace. But it was very clear that because of this disgraceful incident, the Kauravs could never win the war against the Pandavs! You see, again the tenet of *Satyameva Jayate* comes to mind: the victory of truth, which is a central tenet of Indian spirituality.

On the day Draupadi was disgraced, the mighty Bheem swore to drink the blood of Dushasan who had dared lay his hands upon Draupadi. Arjun swore an oath to cut down his oppressors with his fearsome arrows. It is only Yudhishthir who stopped his Pandav brothers from wreaking vengeance on the spot.

So, the victory of the Pandavs was actually concealed within their defeat at the game of dice. Their supposed *defeat led to eventual victory*, because they were walking on the side of right, thereafter. Yes, Yudhishthir made a grave mistake. But afterwards, he strove to do right by Draupadi. He was, after all, known as one who stood for Dharma, doing the right thing by everybody. Now, Karna is actually known as *Danveer* Karna or the great charitable Karna. He has great qualities in him. He's so generous. Yet, all that generosity was given up when he was overtaken with bitterness in his heart.

And it is from this bitterness that we must learn a lesson in order to avoid difficulties as a society.

The root of all conflict is the selfish aims and complexes of man. Karna is a deeply complex person. On the one hand, he gives away his battle armour to Indra, the divine father of Arjun, and thereby depletes his own power upon the battlefield. But on the other hand, he has his own very human frailties.

Dhyaana and Self-Realization

Eventually, the Mahabharat is a sacred text about self-realization, Dhyaana, or meditative oneness with all things. It's about cultivating inner harmony. And this inner harmony is expected of true warriors on the battlefield. You see, the character of war in ancient India was very strange. The enemy was looked at as somebody who would *bring out the best in oneself!* So if you were fighting a brave enemy, you had to respect his strength, his brilliance, his valour—and that way, become united and harmonious in the act of war, evolving oneself. The lesson is this: look at difficult circumstances as opportunities to evolve. In fact, the greater the adversary the more your own self-evolution happens.

This is why Karna and Arjun—placed on two different sides of the human chessboard, so to speak—are regarded as the very paragons of warriorhood. Both bring out the best in each other. Both are full of the light of courage, insight, and higher purpose. Both know that the Infinite has willed them to use their martial skills to do their duty as It sees fit. That is the example we must follow!

The Final Lessons of the Mahabharat

There are several other lessons that the Mahabharat imparts. One of the key things is *achieving societal peace* after the war for justice. And achieving peace of heart, peace of mind, inner peace, peace of soul—these are the takeaways for human beings as individuals. The idea is this: if you make peace within yourself, if you are able to transcend your ego, your circumstances, your difficulties and enmities, your likes and dislikes, then are you able to move on to greater living!

The second ultimate lesson we have to learn is that we must be *reasonable*. We should not be like the Kauravs. The Kauravs, under Duryodhan, rejected all peace proposals. They rejected even Krishna's entreaties for peace. We must take the opportunity we have to make peace with others also, just as we make peace with ourselves.

The third ultimate lesson of the Mahabharat is to *never shirk from a fight for justice*. The war described within the Mahabharat was a tremendously immense one. For the first time, all the kingdoms of the great land of Bharat joined the war, fighting on either side. In fact, the conflict within the Mahabharat is a universal one. It is gigantic in its destruction. Millions perished. But at the end of the day, justice prevails, the Pandavs prevail. So, another lesson is regarding *victory of truth*. Establish yourself in Sat or truth. The Indian texts say that Sat-Chit-Ananda is the ultimate goal of human life. Where there is truth or Sat, you'll find greater consciousness or Chitta. And where there is Chitta, great consciousness, you will find true happiness or Ananda. So the road to Ananda begins from truth!

Yes, the war did consume great warriors, such as Abhimanyu, Drupad, Virat, Iravan, and also the five young sons of Draupadi. From the Kaurav side fell the great patriarch Bheeshma, Drona, Jayadrath, Shalya, Shakuni, Duryodhan, and a multitude of other warriors. In fact, it is said in the Mahabharat that only twelve warriors survived the war (the five Pandavs, Satyaki, Kritavarma, Vrikshaketu, Yuyutsu, Ashwatthma, Kripacharya, and of course, Krishna)! The battle was fought for eighteen days. Karna himself fell on the seventeenth day. Both Karna and Arjun were evenly matched—two great warriors, two separated brothers, two fearless souls equal in their might, in their poise, till the play of karma caused Karna's chariot to become stuck through the maya or mysterious power of destiny. And beholding Karna's predicament, Arjun's divine charioteer—the inscrutable and glorious Krishna—instructed Arjun to release the arrow, thus extinguishing the living light of the radiant earthly son of the mighty celestial Sun God. The great Karna, in all his glory, lost his life like the sunbeams get hidden within the glorious sunset . . . Yet through this very play of loss for most, gain for some, one vital lesson is taught: all "doership" is to be surrendered to the Divine! All is the will of the greater. We must surrender ourselves and play our parts on the battlefield of life (the act of *samarpan*), no matter whether we "win" or "lose" on the material plane.

The next lesson is that *enemies are enemies only on the battlefield*. In ancient India, you could visit each other in friendship after battle hours. In fact, the Mahabharat is so strange! Look at the character of Bheeshma. He's like a godfather to all. He *himself* had hinted the Pandavs about the way to defeat him, when they had requested him to, because the Pandavs found it difficult to emerge victorious and reclaim their kingdom as long as Bheeshma was fighting on the Kaurav side!

The next lesson of the Mahabharat is taught to us through the example of Yudhishthir who, upon knowing that Karna is his eldest brother, wept deeply for him. Yudhishthir looked beyond his personal interest! Sometimes, *you have to see the larger picture*. Even your enemy can be revered. Hence, never give up on somebody. *Never feel that the other person is worthless or useless, even if the other person is opposed to you.* A lot of people undergo difficulties in relationships sometimes because of difference of opinions. Learn to *appreciate* what the other person is and how he/

she thinks. Never think self-righteously in an egoic manner: learn to respect all beings.

Hence, the abiding lesson: learn to *have gratitude for all things*. And gratitude goes with humility. You see, it is a very strange aspect of the Mahabharat that Kunti—even when her sons were taking over the kingdom after their victory in the Kurukshetra war—actually chose to attend to Dhritarashtra and Gandhari who were the enemy's parents, the Kauravs' parents. She encouraged the Pandavs to go and *ask their forgiveness* because they had killed their sons. Kunti decided to be supportive of those who she felt had lost more than her—because Dhritarashtra and Gandhari had lost their own children, *Kunti had compassion for them. So, this idea of compassion, this idea of empathy, this idea of serving those less fortunate than us is indeed a very important one.*

The penultimate lesson of the Mahabharat is that within us, we are capable of choosing from all the opposites of life, all the contradictions of life. It is always your choice. You are capable of the highest love, you are capable of the deepest hate. You are capable of the vastest compassion, you are capable of violent jealousy. You are capable of the greatest insight, you are capable of blind ignorance. Remember, always make the right choice: it is up to you.

The Mahabharat is an echo of all that humanity itself is, and also of that infinite energy which lies beyond humanity, and to whom life and death are mere bubbles upon the ocean of the cosmos. Yet at the heart of the Mahabharat is embedded one final lesson: that of supreme peacefulness. This is truly the message of peace: beyond war, beyond self-conflict or conflict with others. All things must face material destruction, yet even amidst all this we must find peace deep within ourselves. Krishna says in the Bhagvad Gita: "I am become Time, the destroyer of all worlds." Eventually, the Supreme destroys even the vast, the greater, the infinite, all material things and worlds, and refreshes existence with new creation! In that spirit, we must never dread the passing of the old, and *always look at the world and ourselves with deep hope and peace*. Yes, deep within your heart, you can find contentment (*santosha*) and peace (shaanti). As the *Shaanti Mantras* say: "*Om Brahma Shaanti, Antriksha Shaanti, Prithvi Shaanti, Aapah Shaanti, Vishway Shaanti, Vishvedevah*

Shaanti, Vanaspatay Shaanti, Aushadhayah Shaanti, Saama Shaanti, Shantirevah Shaanti, Sarv Shaanti."

Om shaanti shaanti shaanti
Om! Peace, peace, peace

Acknowledgements

I wish to express my humble gratitude to the people who have made this series possible:

Anuj Bahri, my super literary agent at Red Ink.

Shikha Sabharwal and Gaurav Sabharwal, my wonderful publishers at Fingerprint! Publishing, and their team.

Garima Shukla, my amazing and brilliant editor.

Jayden, my loving Godson.

Sri PK Shah, a respected mentor and guide.

Mr Umesh Dwivedi, a teacher, friend and guide over decades.

Gratitude also to my gurus, my parents and entire family, friends, and teachers. Special thanks to my batchmates from SPS, each of whom is a cherished friend. Indraneel Chakravarty and Kuldip Ghosh have been rock-solid in their support over the years, as have all the others! Thank you.

Pranay is a mystic, speaker, and author of several books on spirituality.

Pranay's modules on 'Advanced Spirituality for Leadership and Success' (PowerTalks/MysticTalks) have won global acclaim.

Connect with him on his website: pranay.org